In the Hollow of God's Hand

In the Hollow of God's Hand

"All by grace!"

Roy C. Nilsen

Roy C. Nilsen

ZION PUBLISHING

Copyright © 2004 by Zion Publishing

Cover painting, *Reflections*,
by Kristi Ylvisaker, Sogndal, Norway
Cover design by Karisa Runkel

Edited by Mary Ylvisaker Nilsen
and Solveig Nilsen-Goodin

All rights reserved under International and Pan-American Copyright Conventions. No part of this book may be used in any manner without written permission of the publisher.

Scripture texts are from or adapted from the King James Version, the Revised Standard Version, or the New Revised Standard Version of the Bible.

Library of Congress Control Number: 2004092720

ISBN 0-9627147-2-0

Published in the United States by

Zion Publishing
1500 Crown Colony Court #540
Des Moines, Iowa   50315-1073
1-800-996-2777

www.zionpublishing.org

Printed in the United States of America

PREFACE

THE WONDER OF MINISTRY for me over the past forty years is the privilege I have had to walk with people through the most significant transitions of their lives—birth, baptism, confirmation, graduations, marriage, and, finally, dying. My appreciation for how God's grace works in people struggling to live fully and faithfully in these transitions, or just struggling to live, has deepened as I have witnessed the repeating life cycles of sorrow to joy, pain to healing, discord to peace.

In the Christian community, at the time of baptism, confirmation, or marriage, the words spoken from the pulpit are focused on the whole congregation or a specific group of members. But when we move from one existence to another, from life to eternal life, the community stops, gathers, and takes the opportunity to focus on how God worked in one individual life. The community stops, gathers, and explores what we can learn from a family member or friend who has gone on before us. The community stops, gathers, and struggles with the hard questions, the persistent questions, the questions of meaning and purpose, of plan and ultimate plan.

As I reflect on the time when the community will stop, gather, and reflect on my life, I ask myself how I want to be remembered. What qualities of my life bear witness to the grace of God?

I would hope that gratitude, deep abiding gratitude, will be one of them. For as I survey my life, I am overwhelmed by the uncountable gifts and graces I have been privileged to receive.

This book of hope and encouragement brings together many of those gifts and graces. I think of the thousands of hours I have spent with families through all their life transitions, hours that graced me by deepening and sometimes challenging my faith. Most specifically I recall those times with family members after the death of their loved one, listening as they shared so openly stories and impressions of their parent or child, sister or brother, at a most difficult time. It is those stories that helped me weave with words how each life was held in the hand of God's gracious love.

I want to thank, especially, the family members who have so graciously given permission to print the sermon preached at the funeral of their loved one. I hope this book will bring you joy, as readers come to know and are touched by the life of the wife, husband, mother, father, son, or daughter whom you loved.

The creation of this book would never have happened but for the inspired, generous, and skilled efforts of many people to whom I am deeply grateful. As you hold this book, you will notice first the artistry of Kristi Ylvisaker, my sister-in-law, whose vivid color-filled scenes lend energy and vitality to all of God's creation, whose talent fills our home, and whose artistic painting, *Reflections,* now graces the cover of this book. Also, you will be invited into the book by Karisa Runkel's graphic design—a beautiful blending of color and text. And I am exceedingly thankful to Nancy Jones, Deb Wiley, and Anne Running Sovik for their meticulous reading of the manuscript.

Our daughter, Solveig Nilsen-Goodin, has contributed her time and skill to this project by artfully editing and carefully copyediting each sermon. I am also grateful to all our children—Per, Kai, Linnea, Solveig, and Erika—for their support and love, for committing their lives to ministry in the church and in the world that I so love, but most specifically for their encouragement and advice as the concept for this book took shape.

Finally, Mary Ylvisaker Nilsen, my beloved wife and marvelous companion of nearly fifty years and a gifted writer and publisher, has been the spark behind this project—a gracious encourager and superb editor, who has thoughtfully reflected with me on the lives of the people in this book and the message their lives bring to the rest of us. To her my heartfelt thanks.

Standing at the juncture between life and death gives one pause. One looks both backward and forward and joyfully finds that both are embraced by the grace of God. St. Paul shares this insight, "If we live, we live to the Lord, and if we die, we die to the Lord. So, therefore, whether we live, or whether we die, we are the Lord's." As the inscription on my grandmother's grave reads, "All by grace." How marvelous to rest safe and secure in the hollow of God's hand.

Roy C. Nilsen

TABLE OF CONTENTS

CAROL NOEL, AGE 5
A CHILD SHALL LEAD THEM — **1**

NICOLE, AGE 10
THE GIFT OF JOY — **5**

PAMMY, AGE 22
HARD QUESTIONS, NO ANSWERS — **9**

JOHN MICHAEL, AGE 27
CALLED TO BE A FRIEND — **13**

ABDULA, AGE 30
THE GOD WHO HOLDS US ALL — **17**

GREGORY, AGE 34
THE SIMPLE LIFE — **21**

KENNETH, AGE 37
A RICH AND FULL LIFE — **25**

BARBARA, AGE 40
"I LIFT MY EYES TO THE HILLS" — **29**

STACIE, AGE 42
IF ONLY … — **35**

MAVIS, AGE 45
PRECIOUS MOMENTS — **39**

MARK, AGE 46
*THE UNFAIRNESS OF LIFE — **43***

JEAN, AGE 53
*THE STRENGTH OF THE WEAK — **47***

DON, AGE 55
*A LIFE OF INTEGRITY — **51***

GEORGE, AGE 56
*"LO, I AM WITH YOU ALWAYS" — **55***

JEAN, AGE 58
*"TOUCHED BY AN ANGEL" — **59***

NICK, AGE 61
*YOU TURN OUR MOURNING INTO DANCING — **63***

NANCY, AGE 63
*KNOWING THE WAY — **67***

RUTH, AGE 64
*A LIFE OF FAITHFULNESS — **71***

ART, AGE 65
*STRONG-WILLED AS A MUSKIE — **75***

LILA, AGE 69
*IN QUIETNESS AND CONFIDENCE … — **79***

DONALD, AGE 70
*STRAIGHTFORWARD, HONEST, DIRECT — **83***

BETTY, AGE 73
*THE GIFT OF LOVE — **87***

GINNY, AGE 74
*"ONE DAY AT A TIME" — **91***

DICK, AGE 75
GENTLE STRENGTH — **95**

DON, AGE 75
A LIFE WELL LIVED — **99**

CARROLL, AGE 76
STRONG HANDS — **103**

JAMES, AGE 76
THE PLANS I HAVE FOR YOU — **107**

LEONARD, AGE 79
A BOOK WRIT LARGE — **111**

DONALD, AGE 79
A GIVING LIFE — **115**

GEORGE, AGE 80
FROM ADRIFT TO MOORED — **119**

LESTER, AGE 80
THE PATIENCE OF A FISHERMAN — **123**

PAT, AGE 83
FOR EVERYTHING A SEASON — **127**

GEORGE, AGE 83
THOSE WHO WALK IN WISDOM — **131**

RUTH, AGE 84
A FAITHFUL LIFE. A FAITHFUL GOD — **135**

MAYBELLE, AGE 86
FLOWERS BLOSSOM AND FADE — **139**

DOROTHY, AGE 86
"FOR GOD SO LOVED THE WORLD" — **143**

JIM, AGE 87
A MAN WORTH HIS SALT — **147**

FARRELL, AGE 87
THE DISCIPLINED LIFE — **151**

GLADYS, AGE 89
KEYS TO THE KINGDOM — **155**

ERCELL, AGE 89
"A TIME TO PLANT" — **159**

FRANCIS LEE, AGE 90
HE JUST HAD IT IN HIM — **163**

WEST, AGE 91
THE GIFT OF FAMILY — **167**

HELENE, AGE 91
FROM SURVIVING TO THRIVING — **171**

VAN, AGE 91
A MAN OF STRONG CONVICTIONS — **177**

STELLA MAE, AGE 93
"STILL MORE I'D LIKE TO DO" — **181**

LEORA, AGE 95
A GOD WORTH BELIEVING IN — **185**

IRENE, AGE 95
THE PEACEFUL WEAVER — **189**

RALPH, AGE 95
GOD BE PRAISED! HALLELUJAH! — **193**

MOTHER, AGE 88
IN THE HOLLOW OF GOD'S HAND — **197**

INDEX — **203**

INTRODUCTION

DURING THE SIX YEARS he spent in his first call—a two-point rural parish near Sunburg, Minnesota, population 161—Roy Nilsen was known by the area bishop as "Burying Sam." He preached 138 funeral sermons during those six years, and all of them had to be different. The same people came to every funeral.

Being the only professional in town, Roy was often the first person on the scene in an old farmhouse, witnessing the final death gasps, closing the eyes of the person who had just died, hearing the wails of fresh grief. A heavy burden for a young man just out of seminary.

During those years he discovered the power of that moment when the veil between this world and the next disappears, the power of that moment when God enfolds both the dead and the living in a single embrace, the power of being present in that moment to people in their grief and, with words and touch, proclaiming that death is not the end of the story.

In forty years of ministry, Roy walked with more than five hundred individuals and families through the valley of the shadow of death, listening deeply to the stories and the silence, the wails and the whys, taking it all into his heart, wrapping it all in God's love, and tenderly molding it into a word of hope, an affirmation of life, a proclamation of the Gospel. Over the years, this message has given countless mourners the courage to go on living, the courage to dare to believe that the promise the pastor proclaimed was true: one day their tears would turn into songs of joy and their mourning would turn to dancing.

One cannot traverse the valley of the shadow of death so many times with so many people and not be changed. Indeed, each sojourn into that valley changed and deepened Roy, shaping him into the pastor, preacher, and human being he has come to be.

As a tribute to Roy's life and ministry of four decades, therefore, it seemed fitting to dip into his collection of some five hundred funeral sermons preached over the years and choose a cross section to preserve in this volume. Our criteria for selection had to do primarily with age and gender, as well as the very practical reality that most of the sermons from the last twenty years had been written and saved on a computer. Because of this, the forty-nine sermons in this collection were all preached either at Zion Lutheran Church in Iowa City, Iowa, or at St. John's Lutheran Church in Des Moines, Iowa, or perhaps at a funeral home.

Funerals and memorial services always include more than just a sermon. There may also be an obituary and stories or comments by family and friends. In the editing process, therefore, we occasionally added information to the sermon that had been stated in other parts of the service in order to provide a more accurate rendering of each person's life and death. The final sermon, about the death of Roy's mother, was preached the Sunday after her burial, and therefore he was able to comment on her funeral.

In addition, almost every sermon Roy preached included introductory scripture readings and greetings to family and friends, as well as closing scriptural references to resurrection and life eternal. To respect the privacy of families and avoid redundancy, we removed most of this introductory and closing material, while maintaining the integrity of the sermons themselves along with their proclamation of the Gospel. A complete listing of biblical texts used for each sermon can be found in the index on pp. 203–5.

Finally, we attempted to move the text from spoken to written prose without losing the voice and cadence so evident in Roy's preaching. To that end, we have made extensive use of sentence fragments and other atypical prose style elements.

While funeral sermons are about the person who has died, they are preached for those who are living. These sermons speak in a myriad of ways about the uniqueness and sacredness of each human life. In so doing, they invite us to claim the uniqueness and sacredness of our own lives and to live them abundantly, even joyfully, in the midst of the grief and pain and ordinary messiness of our days.

And these sermons also invite us to look at death in a new way. In a culture that would have us deny and defy our mortality at every turn, this volume provides an opportunity to accompany others into the valley of the shadow of death, much as Roy has done with so many people throughout the years. And in that journey we may indeed discover what Roy has discovered: death is a mystery. But in the presence of God, it need not be feared.

It is our hope that *In the Hollow of God's Hand* honors those whose lives and deaths are recorded in these sermons. We also hope that this volume honors Roy and his forty years of faithful and powerful ministry. But more than anything, we hope that all who read this book will be freed and inspired to live fully and, when the time comes, to die peacefully, trusting deeply the wideness of God's mercy, the faithfulness of God's love, and the assurance of God's promises. For without a doubt, in life and in death, from womb to open tomb, we are held safe and secure in the hollow of God's hand.

Mary Ylvisaker Nilsen
Solveig Nilsen-Goodin

In the Hollow of God's Hand

by
Roy C. Nilsen

CAROL NOEL
AGE 5

HOW MUCH ARE we adults willing to learn from a child? About life? About love? About trust? About joy?

We have heard this afternoon about the absolute delight of Baby Carol, "B.C." as she was called. We have heard of her daily exuberance. Of her laughter and giggling. Of her energy and enthusiasm. Of her love and caring.

We have heard of the daredevil toddler who was unafraid to try anything. Of the free spirit who loved getting naked just like the folks in the Garden of Eden before they were messed up by shame. Of the model who would dress up with her sister Maddy in a feather boa and in jewels to pretend to be ladies. And of the imp who asked a pastor, "Why do you wear a dress?"

We have heard of the kid who loved animals and babies and who more than anything wanted to see a real birth of a baby. Of the kid who loved horseback riding and bike riding and who loved going fast.

We have heard about the brave girl who didn't think open-heart surgery was a big deal and who called her scars "shark bites." And we've heard how great her capacity was to give and receive love. When you held her, she could hold on to you better than anyone. And we've heard that she could draw you into her world and make you feel like a child again.

"I came that my joy may be in you," Jesus said, "and that your joy may be full." And sometimes we adults don't get it. But a little five-year-old gets it. And lives it! How much are we willing to learn from a child?

It was some dour adults who shooed the kids away from Jesus that day when he came to town. And Jesus was upset. "Let them come to me," he told those old fogies. And he held the kids on his knee and in his arms and listened to their giggling and their laughter, their stories and their wonderful worlds of imagination. And he looked into their bright and eager eyes and saw the love in their hearts. And he also saw and delighted in how impish they could be.

A Child Shall Lead Them

Then he asked the long-faced adults how much they were willing to learn from a child.

"This is what the kingdom of God is all about," Jesus says. It is about these kids who love beyond measure, who trust when adults can't, who fly like Peter Pan, who play to the full and then cuddle exhausted in your arms. Somehow they see what God's plan is all about—a plan adults too often forget.

One of the family members told me that not long ago, while they were in the hospital waiting in vain for a heart transplant, B.C. asked if someone would sing her a "God song." And her grandma sang:

Jesus loves me! This I know, for the Bible tells me so.
Little ones to him belong. They are weak but he is strong.
Yes, Jesus loves me. Yes, Jesus loves me. Yes, Jesus loves me.
The Bible tells me so.

Today, that song is a good one, not only for Maddy and the other children here, but for us all. For in this time of hurt, we are weak, but God is strong. In this time of pain, we feel alone, but to God we belong.

And God will get you through. With all your sadness, with all your questions, with all your grief. God will get you through.

For, you see, the power of God isn't the power that

keeps bad things from happening to good people. The power of God is the power of love that helps people get through the bad things.

The power of love will help us celebrate again, if we are willing to learn from a child. Learn to love, to trust, to be filled with joy again. Learn to sing deep in our hearts, "Jesus loves me! This I know."

And one day, this Jesus, who loves us, promises we shall be together again, all of us. And Jesus never, never breaks a promise. Amen

NICOLE
AGE 10

MIKE, JULIA, BRYAN, family members, teachers, classmates, and friends, I bring you grace and peace in the name of Jesus Christ, the resurrection and the life. Amen

First, I want to thank you, Mike and Julia, for witnessing to your faith in Jesus by modeling courage and patience, humility and love, hope and more hope for all of us. I want to thank you because, amid all your fear, all your pain, all your frustrations, all your sadness in these past three years, you were willing to open your lives to us and to invite us to walk with you. This has been a gift beyond measure. I know I can speak for Nicole's teachers and classmates, her coaches and teammates, her neighbors and friends, and for all of us here at St. John's. Our lives have been changed. We are not the same. We have all been blessed because you have allowed us to walk this journey with you.

During Nicole's fight against cancer, the story of Jesus and the children has often come to mind. I picture Nicole as one of the kids responding to Jesus' welcome, strolling toward him with that grand smile on her face, not letting her prosthesis slow her down. I see Jesus lifting her into his lap, giving her a hug, and blessing her, saying, "Nicole, I have given you the gift of joy. Have fun with it. Share it."

And Nicole did. She lived her gift. She took joy in doing everything she could possibly do. She found joy in the neighborhood kids, the school kids, the church kids, the family. She understood what Jesus means when he speaks to all of us about his joy being in us that our joy might be full.

Each of you can remember some marvelous moments when her joy touched you. Those of you who were with her in the Talented and Gifted Program. Those who played with her or against her on the Recreational Basketball team or the Northwest Soccer team. Those who shared a class with her at school or church. Those who saw her paintings or her work in clay. Family, teachers, friends, peers. She touched us with joy.

The Gift of Joy

Here was a girl who, after her amputation, told her folks she still wanted to play basketball and soccer. And she did. And after a second lung surgery, she informed them she wanted to learn to play the flute. And she did. And whether she was playing piano or singing in the chorus or charging down the floor toward the basket or sitting and talking with her mom and dad or grandma and grandpa, we all saw the delight in her.

I will never forget the joy with which she carried the offering plate up to the altar one Saturday evening worship, proud and strong, walking on that prosthesis. Or All Saints' Sunday last year when she received her first communion, all decked out in her blue dress and a look of delight in her face as she eagerly took the bread and wine, the life of Jesus, into her.

Joyful and strong, she was. With a stubbornness that not even the physicians and nurses who treated her could get around, nor any of the rest of us, either. Hers was a determination that told us all, "I believe I'm supposed to live a full life and I will!"

And so we celebrate Nicole's life, a life grounded in God's love, a life that encourages us now even as she encouraged many through the most difficult and stressful times in these past years. She kept us going, when it should have been the other way around.

And now, let me speak to Nicole's classmates. Thank you for loving her and caring for her as you did. Thank you for letting her be herself, even when the surgeries and the chemotherapy and radiation wore her out. Thank you for being her friends. If she could say something to you, I think it might be something like this: "Don't be afraid. Even when bad things happen, don't be afraid. Talk to your mom or dad, or grandma or grandpa about it. Don't be afraid—even of dying. Fight against it with all you have. But don't be afraid.

"Every day, do the things that bring you joy. And share the love your family, your teachers, your friends give you. And remember, God loves you, more than you'll ever imagine. You can count on that no matter what happens."

Friends, God's love is promised to all people. It is a love that brings joy to our hearts. That gives hope for our tomorrows. That assures us nothing will ever be able to separate us from God. And one day there will be no more crying, and no more dying, but only life full. And our joy will be complete. Amen

*P*AMMY
*A*GE 22

IN THE FIRST CHAPTER of Philippians we read, "I am sure that God who began a good work in you will bring it to completion at the day of Jesus Christ."

These past days have been days of hard questions. Why did this car accident happen? Why the ice and sleet and snow just then? Why didn't God prevent this horror? Why isn't life fair? Why do some people have to die so young?

Questions have stalked our every step since the accident, since the desperate hours in the hospital, since Pammy died.

We long to have our questions answered, but we find we are met by silence. The answers don't come. And what are we to do? To give up on the God we thought would give us the answers? To give up on the God who didn't deliver like every one of us here hoped God would deliver?

A few years ago, I wrote these words about a friend, "She dared to ask all the hard questions and had the courage to live without the answers."

My friend tried giving up on God, only to find herself traveling a hopeless road, a road that did not encourage, a way that did not empower. And so, humbly, she vowed to trust God and to courageously live without answers.

When that friend of mine died, I remember being so angry with God that I came home and read aloud the forty-two chapters of the book of Job, expressing my anger as vehemently as Job had expressed his when he lost everything. And when I finished, I felt a strange peace come over me, the peace that follows release of anger. And once the anger was gone, God could begin to bind up my hurts, soothe my wounds, dry my tears, and restore my hope.

As I held Chris for a few moments on Friday, I encouraged him to let his anger out, anger over the loss of his beloved young wife, Pammy. We prayed together for the help he would need and the support and encouragement that would be necessary for him, and for all of you, to be revived and renewed again.

You see, the power of God is not the power to prevent bad things from happening to good people. It's not the

Hard Questions, No Answers

power to keep hurt and pain away from us. It's not the power to allow us to go through life unscathed by troubles. Maybe that's what we would like God's power to be for us, but it isn't. God's almighty power is not the power that keeps bad things from happening. It is the power that gets us through those bad times, the love that embraces us, the hope that helps us go on.

God's almighty power is the power of love. God's almighty power is the power I see in you as you surround Chris and the other family members with love. God's almighty power is the very power of love we all were touched by in Pammy's life.

During these days, you've been talking about how that love showed in so many ways to her family and her friends. How she was willing to share everything with you, not only possessions, but spirit and energy and time. How she could motivate softball and volleyball teams and wrestlers, too. How she could draw the best out of people. How she decorated her home and tended her garden with such loving care. You've told me about her winning smile and her love of fun.

And I remember, during their premarital counseling, after she and Chris had taken a certain test and discovered she was just about off the charts with her organizational and decision-making qualities, how she laughed at her propensity to organize everybody else's life in addition to her own. And somebody told me yesterday that if volleyball is played in heaven, Pammy is already getting some new winning team set to go.

God's almighty power is the power of love and that's what touched us in Pammy's life. And that is why it hurts so much today. We saw that love. We experienced it. And because of that, we found that God's love really does flow through people.

But just because Pammy is gone doesn't mean that love is gone. I see the power of God's love right here, its threads woven together in you to care for, encourage, support, and love one another through your tears, your anger, your fears, your hopes, your dreams. And not even death can take it away.

For the sun will rise tomorrow, and the God of yesterday and today awaits our entry into tomorrow with whatever it will bring. And that same God promises the almighty power of love will carry us through, for God is love and those who live in love, live in God.

As you permit God's love to live in you, then you have this promise, which was the confirmation verse I chose for Chris almost ten years ago: "I am sure that God who began a good work in you will bring it to completion at the day of Jesus Christ." Of this you can be sure. Amen

John Michael
Age 27

FRIENDS, I BRING YOU grace and peace in the name of the risen Christ, who comes to give new life and hope to all who grieve this sudden death and to all the world. John, this son, this friend, this athletic young man who died far from home of meningitis just weeks after returning for his third season of basketball, is no longer with us.

Many of you knew John as friend, on the basketball court or off, at the places where your lives intersected. There was something about him, a niceness, a goodness, a spirit that spoke of the value he placed on those healthy and strong relationships with people—his "mates," as his Aussie teammates might put it.

Friend. A marvelous word filled with images of comfort and care, of security and possibility, of laughter and delight, of love and hope.

Friend. An old word. Anglo-Saxon in origin. A word that has to do with esteem and respect. A word that has to do with the strong bond that holds people in connection to one another. A word that describes how we might live so much more fully and authentically as humans, if our eyes could but see one another as friend, no matter one's station in life, no matter the color of one's skin or the content of one's beliefs, no matter one's politics or lifestyle.

Friend. This old word that has served us so well through the ages is derived, interestingly enough, from a verb that means "to love." A kind of love that is patient and kind, not arrogant or rude. A love that doesn't insist on its own way, that doesn't carry a grudge. A love that rejoices in what is true. A love that is marked with faithfulness and hopefulness and strength. A love that isn't only present for the good times, but sticks with you in the tough times. A love that hangs in there, that doesn't end.

Can you see John in that mosaic of friendship? Can you recognize this tall, hard-playing guy who thought it was a miracle that he received a scholarship to OSU? This fellow who enjoyed being with his parents as much as he did his peers? This free spirit who always seemed to land on his feet? This young man who accepted the difficulties that came his way with, "That's life," and who kept on going? Can you see him in those words in I Corinthians 13, as his mom can?

Friendship. Love. The words belong to each other. That's what Jesus tells us in the Gospel from St. John. "This is my commandment, that you love one another as I have loved you." And he continues, "You are my friends if you do what I command you. I do not call you servants any longer, but I have called you friends, because I have made known to you everything that I have heard from God."

Friendship. Love. Strong words together. Words that lift up. Words that give hope. Words that give life.

Jesus spoke those words to his disciples to help them see that the essence of life is love, and the commandment of God is love. And that to love is to be a friend of Jesus and a friend with Jesus. The good word is that Jesus our friend stands with us and for us, strongly, passionately, joyfully. With us as we journey through life with all its questions that remain unanswered, with all its hurts and grief that would pull us down. But also with us through all life's dreams and visions and wonder, all its delights and just common ordinary pleasures played out on a basketball court or in time spent with family or in sharing one's self with one's friends.

In the Hollow of God's Hand

Today, the risen Christ comes to us to lift us up, to enable us to keep on going during this time of unspeakable grief. But today, Jesus also comes to us so we may continue to celebrate the resurrection by living the life of love that a tall, six-foot-ten fellow named John gave us a glimpse of, a love that we have the privilege of offering one another every day.

Thanks be to God who gives us the victory through our Lord Jesus Christ, who calls all who live in love "friends." Amen

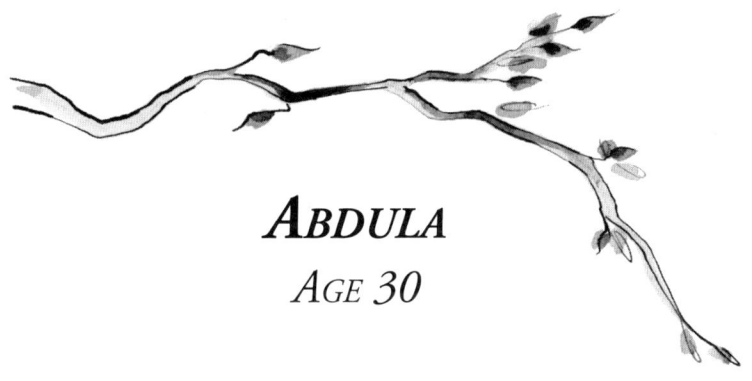

Abdula
Age 30

WE MET ONLY ONCE, Abdula and I. He was sitting on the edge of his bed at the University of Iowa Hospitals. He looked puzzled when I entered his room—I, a complete stranger. But I told him I was his folks' pastor and he invited me to sit.

Our conversation focused on how he was doing—the kinds of distress he was experiencing from the lung cancer he was battling, the treatments he was going to receive in the next days and weeks. It was a friendly conversation. "God be with you," I said on the way out the door. "Thanks," Abdula said. "Thanks, and thanks for coming."

In the Hollow of God's Hand

Lots of words could describe Abdula. Frances, his sister, shared some of those words with me yesterday. "Loving, easygoing, compassionate, dedicated to work, religion, family. He liked to help people," she said with a smile that spoke of her affection for her brother.

I would like to add another word from my one-time conversation with him: trusting. The University of Iowa Hospitals can be a most threatening place for a patient. It is a large, complex maze with almost a thousand physicians and more than seven thousand other employees. Doctors, nurses, residents, interns, and aides run in and out of rooms constantly.

Yet, the look on Abdula's face that afternoon was one of trust, as he talked about the people who were working with him, as he spoke of their recommendations for treatment, as he conversed with me, a stranger to him.

He was trusting. Trust is a key word for believers—Muslim and Christian alike. It is how we hold on to Allah, to God, whose ways are beyond our ways. Trust is how we hold on to a God who promises love and justice. Trust is how we hold on to a God who gives hope and meaning for both today and tomorrow.

It is with that trust that we hold on to a God who seeks to comfort us today. A God who gives us courage to go on even in the most difficult times. Who promises that death

The God Who Holds Us All

will not be the ultimate victor, but that we shall live eternally. Who speaks to the deepest part in us and assures us that as we hold on to God, God is also holding us.

The God who gives us each day also gives us this promise: "I will not leave you or forsake you. I will not leave you comfortless."

When joy is turned to sorrow, when happiness is turned to sadness, when the celebration of life is changed and we find ourselves walking through "the valley of the shadow of death," God is with us.

The God who gives us each day is the same God whose grace is sufficient for each day, whose love is strong enough for each day, strong enough to hold on to us, to bring us a sense of serenity and peace, and to renew us again.

Christians believe that God sent Jesus as a human so that we might know how deeply God loves us. The cross tells us of a love that will spare nothing for humanity's sake. And the empty grave tells us of a love that does not leave us at some tragic end, but rather provides us a hope that is real, a confidence that is sure, a life that is forever. That is God's promise.

Trusting in that promise, we go on from here, knowing that though we die, yet we shall live. For what God has begun in our lives, God will bring to completion for Muslim and Christian alike. And one day we will join in a grand celebration of who we all are in the sight of God—the God who made us all and who holds us all. Amen

GREGORY
AGE 34

As I sat early the other evening with Dick and Bev and listened to them talk about Greg's world, it struck me that in many ways it was a wonderful world: a world of delight, of simplicity, of appreciation for small things. It was a world in which Greg found pleasure and enjoyment, and where others found pleasure and enjoyment in him.

It was a world where Dr. Seuss entertained and delighted him with extraordinary, imaginative characters. Like Star-Bellied Sneeches and Horton who hears a Who and that old Grinch who stole Christmas and the Cat in the Hat. I remember reading those Dr. Seuss books to our kids

In the Hollow of God's Hand

and the awe and joy the stories created. No wonder Greg would sit for hours and insist that Dick or Bev "read, read, read!"

His world was a world where sports entranced him and every team was cheered when they scored, and where excitement reigned supreme when it was Iowa scoring. And TV's *Wheel of Fortune* with all of its letters cast a spell over Greg, as did Disney movies and the game Sorry. CDs provided music on his Walkman and calmness for his spirit. John Denver was his favorite—"Just a Country Boy" who experienced a "Rocky Mountain High." The outdoors also brought Greg pleasure. He loved being outside, whether it was the yard at 119 Friendship or at 1111 Marcy or traveling with his folks.

But most of all, Greg just loved being with all of you. Teasing you, sharing with you, trying to please you. I hope you all know how much you meant to him—especially his folks and family, the staff members and residents at the Systems Homes, and those he worked with at the Nelson Center.

It was about twenty-four years ago that Greg and another boy became the first residents of a Systems Home in Iowa City, an experiment in residential living for those who, for mental or physical reasons, couldn't live on their own. In some ways, those two were pioneers, a part of a

The Simple Life

venture that was to grow and grow and provide safe and rewarding home environments for exceptional people. And Greg would be the first to say thanks for all that has meant to him.

As we gather today, we are very much aware of the difficulties that life may bring to us. There is much hurt and pain that marks our days and that marked Greg's and his family's, too. Life is not all wonder and delight. And yet, we need to always be alert to the signs of wonder and delight amid the troubles of life.

It is those signs that I was eager to share with you about Greg. For in Greg's teasing, in his laughter, in his excitement, in his enjoyment of simple things, God has given us a sign. It is the sign of hope in the darkest moments. The sign of comfort in the presence of trouble. The sign of love in a world that needs love so desperately. The sign of God at work to bring wholeness and joy to us no matter what our circumstance in life. The same sign that Jesus brought as he walked amid hurting people, bringing healing and wholeness, joy and delight.

I didn't know Greg by name on those hazy, fall evenings when my wife and I would take our walk up Washington Street and past the Systems House on the corner of Friendship and Washington. But he became familiar to us. At times he would be outside, near the basketball area, just quiet, enjoying the early evening air. He grinned and we smiled and waved.

I look forward to seeing him again. For the promise to those who are baptized into Christ is, "that as Christ was raised from the dead by the glory of the Father, we too might live a new life, for certainly we shall be united with Christ in a resurrection like his." And there will be wholeness of body and mind and spirit, and such joy and delight unbounded that a "Rocky Mountain High" will pale in comparison to it. For that promise we can all give thanks to God! Amen

KENNETH
AGE 37

"I HAVE FOUGHT THE GOOD FIGHT, I have finished the race, I have kept the faith."

Some live rich and full lives though their years be limited. Our friend Kenn is one of those. And how he made the lives of others rich and full, while he lived his own! That is what faith is all about. Not simply believing in God, but taking seriously God's desire to make the lives of all persons rich and full—in love, in gracefulness, in hope, in possibility.

I wonder how many kids in band in East Greene Community Schools found their lives more rich and full because of a band director who cared for them as persons even as

In the Hollow of God's Hand

he instilled in them the vision of being the very best they were able to be as musicians.

I wonder how many neighbors and friends were touched through the years by Kenn's willingness to pitch in when help was needed, and found in him a ready hand, unafraid to work, eager to assist and to be a friend, one who made the living of their days more rich and full.

I wonder how many times his sought-out counsel and listening ear made the burdens and problems of family members lighter and maybe a bit more manageable, so that the richness and joyfulness of life could be seen again.

I wonder how many times the sound of his trumpet touched the people in whatever church he was playing in and lent a new richness and fullness to worship for people coming together in the presence of God.

I wonder how often his love of spending time at home and being with Betty and Alex in the pursuit of simple pleasures—walking, camping, hiking, doing housework, playing together—enriched and made full their days together.

I wonder how many times this quiet, dignified, well-organized man, meticulously dressed and groomed, enabled grieving folk, who had endured the loss of one they loved, to see that the richness and fullness of life would be possible for them again.

A Rich and Full Life

When brain stem cancer was first diagnosed in Kenn three months ago, his desire was to pursue an aggressive course of treatment that had the best possibility of making the rest of his years as rich and full as possible. Undergoing the harsh and risky treatment plan was not an easy choice. And yet for Kenn, it was the only choice, the only chance for him and his family to have more rich and full years together if the treatment worked.

It was with courage and determination that he faced the situation, even though he found himself becoming more and more dependent on others, even though he was unable to communicate, even though he was forced to endure pain and loss of privacy that was so foreign to his nature.

And yet, even when hope dimmed and possibilities faded, he fought for the possibility to have more years of that rich and full life—for his own sake, but more for the sake of his family. He gave it his best, with all the strength he could muster, until his strength was no more and only good-byes were left to be spoken. And then final peace.

I wish I could answer all the questions that run through the mind of an eleven-year-old when his dad dies. But I can't. All I can do is to look in your eyes and the eyes of your mom and tell you, as Kenn told lots of folks who were grieving, that the richness and fullness of life will be possible again.

In the Hollow of God's Hand

    And I can say that because that is the promise of the God Kenn knew, I know, and you know. The promise of our God whose purpose is to bring life in its richness and fullness to all. And when it is taken away for a time by sadness and hurt, by sickness and death, our God is there to comfort us and work to restore the fullness of life.

    How does this happen? It happens when people like Kenn work to help it happen. Friends of God, I call them. People who cry with us, who listen to us, who walk with us. Friends of God, I call them. People who help us see God at work all around us, working to restore the joy of life whenever it is lost. And working to keep us looking toward tomorrow, the tomorrow of God when the rich and full life of eternity awaits, as God has promised us.

    "I have fought the good fight, I have finished the race, I have kept the faith." Thank you, Kenn, for helping us all to see what it means to live a full and rich life. Amen

Barbara
Age 40

WHEN YOU'VE BEEN to the top of the mountain, it is said, you'll never see the world in quite the same way again. You'll always be looking for a new perspective, a better view. Barb was a mountain climber. She started climbing while working in a national park with Christian Ministries and continued in the Cascade Mountains of eastern Washington at Holden Village.

But the day that was a turning point for her was when a team of eleven, with a hiking guide, took off to conquer Mount Rainier. And after a laborious, exhausting trip that sapped most of the energy she had, Barb stood at the top.

In the Hollow of God's Hand

Some folks look at mountains from afar, admiring their strength and beauty, and only imagining what the attempt would be to scale them. Others put on their hiking boots, pack their gear, and climb—savoring the adventure and being willing to tackle the pain, to endure the hurt, to achieve the heights, to see the world anew.

Barb was one of those.

I wonder how often the words of Psalm 121 beckoned her, engaged her, called her to climb, and in the climbing, led her to discover the One who would be her help. The One who would be her safe footing when things got slippery. The One who would stay awake when she grew weary. The One who would keep her going out and coming in. The One who would keep her life.

She was unafraid to tackle the steep climbs. One doesn't end up with a bachelor's degree, two masters' degrees, and a doctorate by being afraid. And whether she was practicing a difficult Bach fugue on the organ, tackling a dissonant solo piece for clarinet, or mastering an intricate passage of orchestral music in the Quad Cities Symphony, she thrived, energized by the climb.

Some ten years ago, Barb found herself with an especially steep climb before her. After being part of the Christus House Community at the University of Iowa for some time, she moved into a commune of sorts. You know,

"I Lift My Eyes to the Hills"

the radical university kind of stuff. Organic food was the order of every day, she would not so gently remind some of us who paid little attention to nutrition or diet. And Republicans need not even knock on the commune door, unless they wanted to be lectured about the inadequacy of their political perspective.

It was about then that the steep climb became an even steeper one and Barb realized she couldn't do this one alone. Sitting in the church office one day, she said, "I've got a problem. My drinking. I need to join AA. I can't do this alone." Honest words, with life-giving potential. And the climb began. And Barb was never alone. With her was the One who was her safe footing when things got slippery, who stayed awake when she grew weary, who kept her going out and her coming in, who kept her life. And transformation took place at the hands of the One to whom Barb looked.

Soon she began wrestling with the call of the church to ministry and was off to the seminary, where she kept on climbing, making sure to care for herself in order to be able to stretch her mind and tackle the life-and-death issues of the faith, of God's people, of the world, and then figure out how to serve that people, that world, that God.

And she met this fellow there who some of us thought at least looked like a Republican, but it didn't matter any more, even if he was. She loved him, and Doug loved her. And they vowed to a life together. And a life in ministry.

Ministry is not easy, as many here know. But it can be a delight to one who is transformed. And that is what we have seen for these years—seen in Barb's eyes, in her countenance, in her eagerness to speak and live that Gospel. Always trying to balance time for Doug and Eric and herself with the demands of the church: lifting up worship as the focus for the people of Immanuel Lutheran in Camanche in their life together, nurturing those kids and teens of the parish, holding the hands of those who were suffering, sharing a word of hope with those who were dying.

We have seen her transformation because she had been to the top of the mountain and knew this One who climbed with her every step of the way, this One who turns people around, this One who transforms today, this One who promises that one day death shall be no more. And life, she knew, could never be the same again.

No wonder she could so pensively play "Just a Closer Walk with Thee" on that clarinet at one moment and then wail with delight with the Pastors' Polka Band on her favorite, "When the Saints Go Marching In," at another.

God transforms, God gives new life in Jesus Christ. God makes us new. So even when mocked by death, we boldly proclaim that there is one grave already empty.

"I Lift My Eyes to the Hills"

When Barb was diagnosed with cancer, she faced yet one more climb, perhaps her most difficult one yet. The past few weeks of Barb's illness and hospitalization have been painfully hard as we all began to realize that this climb was not going to turn out as we had hoped. But even then there were moments of laughter and delight, of faithful singing and hope that would not be diminished, of healing of the spirit, if not of the body, of confidence in a faithful God, present and lovingly caring for Barb and Doug and Eric and this family. And at the end there was a marvelous sense that God had finally carried Barb to the mountaintop. And now it is we who will never see the world in quite the same way again.

"I lift up my eyes to the hills—from where will my help come? My help comes from the Lord, who made heaven and earth." And so we press on, climbing our mountains too—sometimes reluctantly, sometimes eagerly, but always with One at our side who is our safe footing when things get slippery, who stays awake when we grow weary, who keeps our going out and our coming in, who keeps our life for eternal life.

In this One we delight. In this One we find courage to press on for the climb still ahead! Amen

STACIE
AGE 42

JESUS CAME INTO the world to bring joy to humanity. Jesus came into the world so that the joy in him might be in us, and that our joy may be complete.

Time after time we see it as Jesus enabled the blind to see, the lame to walk, the deaf to hear. As he healed the lepers, loved the loveless, played with the children, comforted the grieving. All those who had lost joy in their lives found it restored again as Jesus shared himself, his love, his closeness to God and his delight in living.

Look at Stacie's smile on the bulletin cover. Notice how it engages you. It reflects a love of life, a joy that was deep in her.

In the Hollow of God's Hand

You saw that joy in her friendship, in her loyalty, in her fun-loving ways. Some of you knew it because of a love of music that you shared. Some saw it in her delight in horses and riding, or her care for all her pets, or her love of flowers and gardens. Some sensed it in the care she so generously gave to older people—especially the ninety-four-year-old woman she had just begun to care for a short time ago.

A few of you knew it because you knew of her daily prayer life, a lifeline for her as she struggled against those forces within that would destroy her. And those closest to her knew it by the love she had in her, which she shared so generously.

There was a joy there, in spite of Stacie's struggle with health issues, her losing battle with addictions, her repeated life disappointments, especially the death of her beloved father some eight years ago—a death that devastated her. Perhaps that is why the song she loved, "Over the Rainbow," is such a poignant metaphor, hauntingly expressing her wish for that place "where troubles melt like lemon drops," and plaintively asking, "If happy little bluebirds fly beyond the rainbow, why, oh why, can't I?" She longed for joy to be restored.

Joy always looks to be restored when its luster is tarnished, its energy diminished, its fullness depleted. And that is why we are here. And that is why Jesus is present

If Only ...

today. Jesus tells us that he has come to us "so that my joy may be in you and your joy may be complete."

Whether through failures of the medical system, combined with complex physical and emotional problems and addictions, as in Stacie's case, or for other reasons, whenever someone dies at a young age, family and friends start to think of what they could have done or should have done. They often beat themselves up about their failures: If only I had said this. If only I had done that. I've seen it happen so often in the almost forty years I've been working with people in times of death.

But, you know, that kind of thinking is not of God. In fact, it is the biggest roadblock to God's desire to restore joy in our lives. It implies we had the power to be in control, when we never did have that power. It keeps us in the center of our thinking and forces God to the periphery. It focuses on what cannot be changed, instead of what can be.

What *is* of God is to hear Jesus' word inviting us to love God and one another, inviting us to let the joy that is in Jesus Christ enter us anew: The joy that delights in knowing that God is for us, not against us. The joy that delights in claiming the promise that God will bring peace to troubled and broken hearts. The joy that delights in the word of hope that though we die, yet we shall live. The joy that

In the Hollow of God's Hand

affirms, "Nothing can separate us from the love of God in Christ Jesus." Nothing!

We know we can claim this joy because God is present with us and will enable the family and all of us who are grieving to walk again with sure step, freed of thinking, "If only …," delighting in life's goodness, and thankful for the journey. And we will be confident of that day spoken of by Martin Luther King, Jr., August 28, 1963, when Stacie was but three years old: "that day when all of God's children … will be able to join hands and sing … 'Free at last! Free at last! Thank God Almighty, we're free at last!' " And our joy will then be complete.

Thanks be to God who gives us the victory through our Lord Jesus Christ. Amen

Mavis
Age 45

WE SAW THEM EVERYWHERE in Mavis and Joe's home. "Precious Moments" of every kind. Mavis collected them. Hundreds of them. Some even in boxes not yet opened. When the kids were little and even when they got big, they knew their name would be mud if they broke any of those "Precious Moments."

Today, as we gather, still numb from the reality of how quickly the ALS brought Mavis low, how quickly the abilities of her body vanished, how quickly we have been left alone, we need to remember that her life is defined not solely by these last months in which the disease ravaged her, but by the precious moments shared through the years. Collectors' items for the heart.

She had this smile that would warm your soul. I could see it from across the Mercy Hospital cafeteria or a few tables away in the Zion parish hall. It welcomed you. It let you know you were important. It let you know she cared about you. I guess that's why her kids said they knew it was just about inevitable: right when they were ready to leave church or a party or the store, Mavis would find another five people she hadn't talked with for a while. And her smile would invite them in. And the kids would shake their heads and the waiting would begin.

If you ever saw Mavis at a University of Iowa women's basketball game, there was never a doubt whose side she was on. Coach Lee and the whole team knew it. She was a Hawk fan. A fan of the first order. Enthusiastic. Excited. Committed.

Her days and years were marked by those precious moments: square dancing, working with the Beta Sigma Phi Sorority, playing euchre, eating raspberries, admiring roses, getting to church.

There was something about her—spirited, yet even tempered; flexible, yet sometimes stubborn to a fault. She was faithful and hardworking, and would give one hundred percent, nothing less.

I suspect her children won't soon forget the time she tried to talk the cop out of giving her a speeding ticket, because she just needed to get them to bed, they were so tired. Or her insistence on spooning chicken soup down them when they were sick (or played sick) and stayed home from school. They still hate chicken soup. Or the smiley faces Mavis would draw on the Band-Aids she applied to their cuts. Or the times she told them she loved them—words the world needs to hear and we need to speak much more often than we do.

I can still see her holding on to the railing on the church's west porch one afternoon, walking up the steps with difficulty. She had come from the hospital to ask me to pray for a friend who was seriously ill. It took her a long time to make her way back to Mercy. But her friend was that important to her.

Mavis and I had lots of conversations about her life, about the tough times, about the good times, about the God she believed in, about the hopes she had, even when those hopes had to be scaled back. And about Joe and all he was doing for her and the kids, and how important he was to her.

"Are you afraid?" I asked her not long ago. "No," she answered. "I know God loves me." I didn't push it. I just savored that precious moment with a sister in Christ who

In the Hollow of God's Hand

was giving her witness as she battled with a relentless enemy that would take her life.

Amid all of our questions today, and the hurt we feel because of the loss we've had, and all the precious moments we remember, a word comes to us strong and clear—God loves us. And nothing can ever separate us from that love, no matter how bad the hand we are dealt in life, no matter how difficult the road.

God loves us. God is for us. God is with us. And we'll get through. The precious moments remembered will help us, will encourage us. But it is our Lord who will cause us to remember that the light follows the darkness and morning follows the night. And the One who is the light journeys through the darkness with us. That is the promise of Christ who breaks no promises. Amen

MARK
AGE 46

WELCOME TO YOU ALL. I am glad you have gathered here to remember Mark and also to show your support for Gail and the family. These coming weeks and months will be filled with the pain of their loss and also the rebuilding of their lives. Your prayers for them every day will be important. Your visiting with them and encouraging them will be critical. Thank you for being here today and for what you will do for them and with them in the coming months.

Mark was a big man with a big heart. Coworkers and friends and neighbors knew it. And family especially knew it, because they experienced his love and his care. From the

In the Hollow of God's Hand

surprise for Gail just a little over a week ago on their twentieth wedding anniversary to the cuddling on his lap of Anthony, his grandson, as they watched TV westerns together. He was a big man with a big heart.

It showed in the pride he had in all his kids and in how he talked about them. You all gave him such delight. That is why he enjoyed coaching his sons in baseball so much and was such a strong supporter of Chanel and Mark Jr. in the ROTC program. And why he had such fun watching Lynn and Mike at Tae Kwon Do.

Oh, you kids may have had your run-ins with him. I sense some of you are pretty strong-willed like he was. But his concern to know where you were and what time you were coming home was simply a sign of a protective dad who loved his children deeply.

But Mark wasn't a big man with a big heart whose care stopped at the family's door. His activity in the Masonic Lodge, in the ZaGaZig Shrine and the Mounties, his willingness to help support the Shrine Hospital programs that helped so many children with medical problems, and his service in the Vietnam War tell us of a commitment he had to the larger human family, a commitment more folks in our world could use a healthy dose of.

Yes, his big heart, his love for family and friends, his unswerving loyalty to John Elway and the Broncos, and his

The Unfairness of Life

willingness to stand up for you all were wonderful gifts to you. Your lives have been enriched and strengthened by his.

But there is a hard reality we face today. It is unfair that one who was able to give so much has died at such a young age. Our hearts are filled with terrible pain because of it, and our sense of loss runs deep. We question the wisdom of the doctors who sent him home after his heart attack. We want to stop him from walking up those stairs. We want to do something, anything, to prevent the massive heart attack that ended his life.

So, we are feeling not just pain and loss, but also anger. Anger toward the hospital, but also against God because all this has happened. That anger, to a greater or lesser degree, is in each of you today because you are hurting so badly. Let it out. Let it out in your tears. In your words. In constructive physical ways that don't hurt people or property. You need to.

Mark Jr., at the hospital on Tuesday, your Mom said to you, "You are now the man of the house." I told you that I saw that strength, that ability, in you. And your girlfriend affirmed it. As you let the anger go, more and more you will grow into that role. Then you can be the man with a big heart like your Dad.

We look at the world, we experience our pain, we

discover the world is not fair. That is a truth that has been a part of life since the first people walked away from God in the Garden of Eden, as the story tells us. And that is why we need to know that God is for us, not against us. That is why we need to know that God also has a big heart and God promises to love us to the end.

God doesn't stack the deck against us or against anybody else. God simply says, as you live in an unfair world, I am with you. I will never leave you. I will help you through so that your strength may be renewed like the eagle's, so that you will soar high once again.

And then, one day, standing with all whom we love who have gone before us, we will see God face to face. That is the promise: "Though we die, yet we shall live," for Jesus Christ is the resurrection and the life. Amen

Jean
Age 53

IT HAS BEEN twenty-three years of sobriety for Jean. Twenty-three years of walking one day at a time. Twenty-three years of a life with God, of a life that has grown and flourished and brought joy and love to family, friends, and troubled souls alike.

As many folks in Alcoholics Anonymous do, she shared with me some of her journey the very first time I sat with her in her hospital room as she battled her cancer. Maybe she was so free to talk because she knew about our son's battle with drugs and recovery and our involvement in family treatment, and so she felt in me a kindred spirit.

In the Hollow of God's Hand

I remember leaving her room that day, thankful for her candor, thankful for her spirit, thankful for her—an honest, classy, spiritual woman, whose life had been transformed and continued to be transformed for all those twenty-three years.

Perhaps her walking garden at home is a metaphor for Jean's life. Working hard, willing to spend long hours and do difficult labor with Kirk, she transformed a yard into a walking path, a place of beauty, a spot of serenity, a graceful garden, a place of refreshment and renewal to bring delight to the eye and to the soul.

It has been many years now since Jean found herself weak and discovered God who is strong. It has been many years that God has been at work in her, creating a life of beauty and love and care. And you who have known her—family, friends, coworkers, AA members, church members—have been the beneficiaries of God at work in her life. God gave her love for her own life, and, therefore, she brought joy and love to yours.

Some of you experienced it as she sat you down for a gourmet dinner served with elegance on her best china. You saw it in her ability to turn the ordinary into the extraordinary. Others recognized it in the love she poured out to children and to folks in need. Others witnessed it in her love of hard work and fulfilling her commitments. Still

The Strength of the Weak

others were touched by it at her AA meetings after a long day of work.

Two weeks ago, when I visited Jean in the hospital, she was very weak. We spent about fifteen minutes together. The leukemia and treatment had made her so tired, so worn out. But she was still strong enough to hold on to hope for the bone-marrow transplant in Omaha. She was still strong enough to hold on to hope that her cancer would go into remission. But she was weak. And when I offered to pray with her, she thanked me and said, "It's God who gives me strength." And so we called on God, as she had done so often, so many times, to give her the strength she needed.

"Whenever I am weak, then I am strong." St. Paul's words describe for us what every AA member I've ever met knows: It isn't your strength that gets you through. It is your weakness that allows you to call on God's strength. And that is how you make it.

That's how your life gets transformed—not by your power, but by God's. That's how you become strong, by holding the hand of the One who is strong for us all. That's how your life, too, can become that beautiful garden, where people can see vitality and energy, joy and care, love and goodness, and especially hope growing. And so inspired, they are able to go on.

Today, you may find yourself as weak as you've ever

In the Hollow of God's Hand

been. The loss of one you love does that to you. And today, the same God, whom Jean knew so well, promises to be with you and give you strength. That same God invites you to trust that Jesus' grace is sufficient for you and that his power will be made perfect in weakness. That same Lord says to all of us, "I am the resurrection and the life," and "because I live, you will live forever."

That is the promise of God to Jean and to us all. Thanks be to God! Amen

*D*ON
AGE 55

FROM THE PEN of the psalmist these words: "Give judgment for me, O Lord, for I have lived with integrity ... Test me, O Lord, and try me; examine my heart and my mind. For your love is before my eyes; I have walked faithfully with you."

I can still hear Don speak the words, "The body of Christ given for you." They fell with gentleness from his lips as he placed the bread in my hand. I can still feel the awe in his voice and eye as he handled this gift of grace.

I can still hear the heart of the poet in his prayers that ushered us quietly and confidently into the presence of God at the beginning of worship.

In the Hollow of God's Hand

In those moments we were marked afresh with the presence of the Almighty who calls us to be whole and live holy lives.

"I will live with integrity," said the psalmist. Integrity. Such a life has to do with honesty and purity and uprightness. But it also has to do with soundness and undividedness. It has to do with completeness, with bringing together, with forming into a whole. It has to do with an integrated life—bringing together the body and mind, the emotions and spirit, the private and public, the seen and unseen, the revealed and hidden.

A life of integrity, then, is a life savoring, seeking, searching, pursuing wholeness in relationship to one's self, one's sisters and brothers in the human family, one's environment, one's God.

It is this witness Don so profoundly revealed as he stretched his mind in pursuit of truth and helped other academics and students stretch theirs through the perceptive books and articles he wrote and the classes he taught. As he struggled to know the God who knew him and sought to walk humbly with that God. As he cared for and loved those closest to him—his wife and children. As he included many others in his spirit of gentleness.

Don's life of integrity could also be seen as he tackled the challenge of lawn and garden. As he gave us his own statement on physical conditioning, weaving his way through traffic, uphill and down, in weather good and bad, on that trusty Raleigh bike. As he lifted the level of so much academic conversation with his dry humor. As he affirmed or encouraged an idea from us with a slight nod of his head or a soft expression of "Ah, ah."

Don could be stubborn and seemed downright old fashioned and even stodgy and set in his ways, leading Judy to sigh, "Oh, Don." Perhaps this rigid streak followed him from his former Presbyterianism or he picked it up in his current Lutheranism. Who knows which.

But Don lived as a person of integrity, an integrity born of a simple, yet critically probing faithfulness in a God of integrity. A God faithful to the promises given the human family generation after generation. A God calling us to wholeness of body, mind, spirit, and community. A God from whom all things commence and toward whom all things proceed.

Today we mourn because Don's life was cut short by a massive heart attack just after finishing a lecture to one of his classes. We mourn because we have been robbed suddenly of one who loved us and whom we loved, who respected us and whom we respected, who labored to integrate faithfulness into all of life's relationships and tasks. Death is no friend this day.

But we know that death has only the penultimate word. There is an ultimate word. It comes to us in the words of the Gospel, "I am the resurrection and the life. He who believes in me, though he die, yet shall he live."

What is the sign that this is so? The sign is this, in the words of Protestant theologian Paul Tillich: "In this vast graveyard of the world, we are here to say, 'There is one grave already empty.'" Because Christ lives, we too shall live. Thanks be to God. Amen

GEORGE
AGE 56

I'VE NEVER MET George and yet I feel I know him. It was some four years ago, shortly after I arrived in Des Moines, that we shared the first of our letters. I had had the funeral for his father and sent George a copy of the funeral sermon. We shared a couple of letters with one another.

George had been in prison for a while in Missouri. And yet he wrote of how good he felt because he knew clearly that God was with him. He knew deeply that God loved him. He knew with profound assurance that he was a child of God. And he was at peace in spite of being imprisoned for so many years, an imprisonment he and others felt was

In the Hollow of God's Hand

unjust. He felt so loved by his sister and her family and by friends. For George, life was good.

I remember asking myself after reading his first letter how one could be that content, that serene, while living in prison. And it came clear to me again—what is important is not what is going on around us, but what is going on inside of us.

George, I understand, had a way with the young. He appreciated nature, the creation, the outdoors, and found it easy to talk about it with the young guys. He loved to tease and was ready to give advice to the teen girls in the family about dating and boyfriends.

In prison, George became a counselor to other inmates, helping them sort things out, encouraging them to think in new ways, guiding them through the Twelve Steps of Alcoholics Anonymous, seeking to get them ready to live differently in the future from how they had lived in the past, wanting them to find a better life.

The Third Step of the Twelve Steps is, "We make a decision to turn our will and our lives over to the care of God as we understand him." As I reflect on George's life, it seems to me that what we find in George is someone who did just that. Who found in turning his life over to God a way to live fully even in a most trying situation. Who let God direct him in his concern for others. Who discovered what many do not—how to live fully, compassionately, humbly, joyfully.

In his first letter to me, George wrote that you, his family, taught him more than any others what love and caring were all about through your once- or twice-a-month visits, your weekly letters and calls, your care of George's Missouri home. I mention that today because I know George would want me to. And I also mention it because it demonstrates how each of us has the ability to touch another's life for good. And how that person can influence someone else for good. And on and on it goes. That, too, is a part of the Twelve Step way of life.

Today, we are sad because George died at too early an age. The heart he had turned over to God, the heart filled with love and caring for his fellow inmates, simply gave out one day. But let us go from here knowing that we can make the most of however long we have to live by living fully one day at a time, by turning our will and our life over to God, and by holding on to Jesus' promise, "Lo, I am with you always."

Jesus has also promised, "I am the resurrection and the life." "Because I live, you shall live also." On this day, as we come face to face with death, we do so confidently, knowing that Jesus, who has gone before us from death into life, will come again and claim us as his own.

In the Hollow of God's Hand

And now may the peace of God that passes all understanding keep your hearts and minds in Christ Jesus. Amen

*J*EAN
*A*GE *58*

TOUCHED BY AN ANGEL was a Sunday evening TV favorite of ours when our children were home. It spoke to us of how God works often in mysterious ways, catching us off guard, prodding us to live fully, caring for us through all our days.

Maybe we accepted the show's premise because we grew up with the idea of guardian angels watching over us. "All night, all day, angels watching over me, my Lord; all night, all day, angels watching over me."

Jean knew about angels. She would tell family and friends how angels were watching over them, and how she knew,

In the Hollow of God's Hand

on one occasion, that an angel had saved her from a serious accident. In fact, you might have seen Jean wearing angel jewelry or you might have received a gift from her wrapped in angel paper. And, of course, visiting in their home, you found rooms graciously decorated with angels.

Angels come in many forms and shapes in the Bible and arrive at all sorts of times. They appear to Abraham of old. They announce the birth of Jesus. And one or more, depending on the Gospel you read, tells of Jesus' resurrection. We read of them in depictions of heaven. And we find them described, too, as human beings, whom we may entertain as "angels unaware."

In the Bible, angel simply means messenger—messengers of God who take many shapes, who do many tasks, who communicate the presence, the care, the love, and the wonder of God.

A particular angel named Jean was God's messenger in the most unusual places: In the bank, where Jean tried to understand what it meant to walk in another's shoes and worked hard to get loans for people in special need. In the kitchen, where she prepared a new dish to share with family or friends. On the dance floor with her favorite partner, tripping the light fantastic with delight on her face. On the front steps of the house, sending a child off to college, loving him enough to let him go. In the church, singing her heart out about a God she knew loved her. In the yard at the house, turning it into a garden of beauty, a feast for the eyes. In the house, teaching friends and family to crochet, to knit, to cross-stitch, or to make bracelets for Breast Cancer Awareness. With her family, giving guidance and counsel, sharing her wisdom and her trust in God.

Angels are messengers of grace and goodness, of hospitality and hope, of laughter and love, of compassion and care, of faithfulness and friendship. And Jean was one of them.

We all saw the spark in her, the fun, the enjoyment, the faithfulness, the hope. There would be no giving up for her from the time of the diagnosis that she had inflammatory breast cancer. She would fight that, too. Tears were part of the struggle. And the sadness that comes with them. And yet, to all of us she showed strength, determination to fight, a will to live, trust in God.

She was able to deal with today, not tomorrow; with what is, not with what might be. To embrace now with all its possibilities, all its delights, all its love, all its people. To enjoy the life one has, the moments one lives, the people who cross one's path today.

Someone in the family wrote, "I know that Jean is with God now and that we have a new angel in heaven." The reality is that Jean, in her marvelously spirited way, didn't wait to die to become angelic. Rather, she took seriously that we are all called to be messengers of God, angels, if you will, in our lifetimes. Not the kind of angels that are pious, goody-goody folk, who are so heavenly minded they are no earthly good. But folk who are in touch with heaven and earth, folk who appreciate that God lives among us, that God is very earthy and strong and loving and present in Jesus Christ who, especially during this Lenten season, calls us to conform our lives to his.

Jesus, the great messenger from God, is with us today, bringing us the good news that death hasn't carried this day any more than death carried the day on that Good Friday, long ago. For "Sunday was a-comin'!" And while for Roland and family it seems like it's Friday now, Sunday's a-comin'! Easter is on its way.

That's why we keep going. For we know that because he lives, we shall live also, today, tomorrow, forever. That's the message of the angel. Thanks be to God who gives us the victory through our Lord Jesus Christ. Amen

Nick
Age 61

Nick was a quiet and gentle man who knew how to, as we used to say, "cut a rug." Nick was a dancer. He loved dancing. Holding his partner, gliding across the floor. Enjoying himself and the person who danced with him. His first date with Darlene was spent dancing at the Surf Ballroom in Clear Lake.

Nick was always ready to "trip the light fantastic," as the old saying goes. With his wife, with his daughters, with his grandkids. He was light of foot, had a sense of rhythm, and took pleasure in moving to the music.

The Bible does not contain an abundance of passages

In the Hollow of God's Hand

that speak about dancing. But the few that do use dancing as a metaphor for release, for joy, for delight, for happiness, for victory.

When the people of Israel were led by God from Egypt, they crossed the Red Sea. And when all of the people had come safely to the shore on the other side, immediately the people began to celebrate. And we are told that Miriam and others took tambourines in their hands and began to dance. They sang, "Sing to the Lord, who has triumphed gloriously; horse and rider he has thrown into the sea." And they danced the night away.

In Psalm 30, at the dedication of the temple, the writer speaks of sadness being turned to gladness and mourning being turned to dancing.

There is something of joy that can be seen in dancing—gracefulness and delight, too. That joy, that delight, was what we saw in Nick, whether he was on the dance floor, or singing a song to his kids or grandkids, or playing with them, or watching a sporting event with them, or just holding them in his lap. There was something about him—something playful, something caring, something protective, something deep, something that said, "I love you."

My sense is that Nick's love came through so strongly to family and friends because he knew that he was loved, because he had a sense that God cared deeply about him,

You Turn Our Mourning into Dancing

because he believed God gave everything for him and he could do no less for those around him.

During his long battle with brain cancer, whenever I gave Nick communion in the hospital, I noticed his large hands. Hands that had seen lots of work. Hands that had been joined together in prayer. Hands that had gently held a dancing partner. Hands that had held the hands of the wife, the kids, and the grandkids he loved. Hands that were strong, that made others feel safe and secure.

On my desk I have two pictures of hands. One of them pictures hands at prayer, portrayed by an Ecuadorian artist. These hands are clenched together tightly as if pleading for the suffering of the world. The other is a depiction of God's hand holding a child, with the quote from Isaiah 49:16, "I have held you in the hollow of my hand."

Today, it is the strong hands of God that hold you. In this time of grieving, you are not left alone. In this time of sadness, you are not left to yourselves. In this time of loss, you are not forsaken. "I am the resurrection and the life," Jesus tells us.

Suffering and death come to us all, but they are not the final victors. No, the final victory is resurrection and eternal life. The final victory is the one promised to all God's children. The final victory is the one that danced in Nick's heart, the one found in the love of Jesus Christ for us all.

In the Hollow of God's Hand

And this Christ promises that though we die, yet we shall live, and that nothing can ever separate us from the love of God in Jesus.

It is to those promises that Nick held. It is by those promises that this gentle and trusting man lived, those marvelous promises of God to us all. And I'm here to say, God never breaks a promise.

Today we are mourning, but one day soon, with the psalmist we will say, "You have turned my mourning into dancing and clothed me with joy."

Thanks be to God who gives us the victory, and who tells us we are held always safe and secure in the hollow of God's hand. Amen

NANCY
AGE 63

IT WAS ABOUT supper time, a week ago yesterday, when I walked into Nancy's hospital room. She was alone sitting in the chair beside the bed. She wasn't struggling for breath as I had seen her doing before, but she was very tired. The rapidly growing lung cancer was taking its toll. I didn't plan to stay long. She needed her rest. But just a few moments into the conversation she said, "I need to start planning my funeral soon. Maybe next week when Jean McKinney gets back in town. She's got the forms to fill out for what I'd want in the service."

She sat silently, then, her eyes telling me her thoughts

In the Hollow of God's Hand

were far away. "Nancy, are you afraid to die?" I asked. She shook her head a bit and said, "Pastor, I'm not afraid of death. It's the process leading up to it that's so hard." We talked a few minutes more, and then prayed together, especially for God's help with the dying part, and with thanks for the resurrection that is promised.

"I'm not afraid of death," she told me. It was because Nancy knew the way.

She was one who always seemed to know the way.

When I first arrived at St. John's and wondered where to have lunch downtown, Nancy gave me directions to every restaurant within walking distance. "There's Scruffy's on Fifth and Grand," she told me, "and the Coffee Shop at the Savery Hotel, and Stella's Diner in Capital Square on the second floor, and the Marriott, and the food courts on the skywalk, and of course, Younkers, for food or for shopping." Nancy knew the way.

She knew the way to grow things, plants and flowers of all kinds, at least one hundred different species. And the way to crochet and embroider. And the way to do the jumble puzzles. And the way through that neighborhood where she and Gary lived and where she walked miles most every day. She knew the way to live a full life.

And Nancy knew the way to people's hearts. As spouse and mom and grandma who loved every moment with family. As election judge at Merrill School for years and as receptionist and membership secretary here at St. John's, she could remember names and faces and circumstances of people's lives. "St. John's' corporate memory," Nancy and Virginia were called. And she remembered because she knew how important hospitality is. She was really glad to meet you—whoever you were—and engage you in serious conversation or in banter, with praise or barbed wit, with caring as a Stephen Minister or love as a teacher of kids or delight as a communion visitor. She knew the way to people's hearts.

"I'm not afraid of death," she said. Because she knew the way, the truth, the life. Jesus is the promise of God to whom she held fast, the One who has told us, "I go to prepare a place for you, and I will come again, and take you to myself, so that where I am, there you may be also."

"So, do not let your hearts be troubled, today," Jesus says. "Believe in God. Believe also in me." That's not an order. It's an invitation.

That invitation today is an encouragement to every one of us, for nary a day passes when we don't face a loss of some magnitude. That invitation is an encouragement to every one of us in those moments when we face our own mortality. An encouragement from God who is not far off, but who has drawn near to the world and to us in Jesus

In the Hollow of God's Hand

Christ. And Jesus promises to walk with us and embrace our lives in his own and to hold us fast and show us the way.

That invitation is an encouragement from God who has come today, especially in the bread and wine, the body and blood of Christ, to make us strong and to keep our eyes focused on the One who is the way, the One who loves us with a love beyond measure.

In the words of poet Edwina Gateley, "Let your God look upon you. That is all. God knows. God understands. God loves you with an enormous love. God only wants to look upon you with love. Let your God love you."

And Jesus says to Nancy's family and friends, "Peace I leave with you. My peace I give to you. I do not give to you as the world gives. Do not let your hearts be troubled, and do not let them be afraid. I am the way and the truth and the life."

And so, in the words of the hymn we are about to sing, we call out to Jesus, who is the way, "Take my hand, precious Lord, lead me home." Amen

Ruth
Age 64

Jesus calls us to care for one another in this life, and especially to care for the children. Ruth caught on quickly to this invitation to adventure—and she gave her life to it. The children saw it, as she nurtured their lives. As she celebrated their marvelous inquisitiveness. As she saw each one as beautiful. As she cared for their hurts and helped them to discover more and more of what was in them and around them.

"One of the best third grade teachers there ever was," said a student at Lucas Elementary School. It was an endorsement that made Ruth blush, but was well deserved.

In the Hollow of God's Hand

Her colleagues would say the same as they saw her work and knew the commitment to excellence that lay behind it: In the care she took for the smallest detail. In the lesson plans she designed. In the confident, quiet way she had about her as she cared for and taught the children.

Ruth was faithful. In her profession and to her calling. "Teaching is my life," she shared often with those close to her. She believed God led her to Iowa City to be a friend to children—and to be a friend to many more as well.

At Zion we have witnessed her faithfulness in receiving the Word and Sacrament. We have taken note of her inquisitiveness in Bethel classes and the Book Bunch and in other studies. Ruth was always growing, always stretching, always cultivating that relationship God had begun with her through the waters of baptism.

And somehow that meant we were growing too, those of us who knew her—growing in our understanding of grace, in our appreciation of excellence, in our commitment and faithfulness.

In a prayer book given to Ruth on her confirmation day the short verse from I Thessalonians 5:17 was noted, "Pray unceasingly." Prayer was a sign of her greatest commitment to those she knew and worked with and worshiped with. For when the lesson plans were well prepared and ready to go or the homework gone over and ready to be

A Life of Faithfulness

returned, when the teachers' meeting ended or the church meeting concluded, Ruth's commitment went right on, her commitment for the world, for the children, for us all.

Unbeknown to most of us, she spent forty-five minutes a day ushering us before God's throne of grace in prayer. She brought to God tough situations she needed to work through. And quietly and confidently she trusted God to work. But she didn't look for instant answers. She simply understood that we humans need to know it doesn't all fall in our laps. God is at work doing good in this world.

A few days ago, as I sat at her bedside singing, I asked her what hymn she might like. She whispered, "Germany." For a few moments I was at a loss. Then I remembered the hymn that she and a number of Zion members sang all over Germany on Zion's trip in 1980. I started to sing, "My hope is built on nothing less than Jesus' blood and righteousness." And as difficult as it was for her to sing, in that late stage of cancer that had taken over her body, she sang quietly too.

That was what Ruth's life was really all about: faithfulness to this One in whose name is life and hope, mercy and forgiveness, wholeness and love. This One called Jesus has promised us not an easy life, but an abundant and full life, and has vowed to journey with us.

This is not always easy to believe as we live in a world

In the Hollow of God's Hand

where people of every age suffer and die and we mourn the death of this good woman to pervasive cancer. God seems strangely absent in such a world. And yet, possibly, we need new eyes to see—the eyes of children not clouded by adult sophistication and rationality and cynicism. Eyes possessing instead the clear vision of simple trust.

In this way Ruth was one with the children of the world and shared their wisdom. "For to such belong the kingdom of God."

She told me once that she couldn't remember a time when she didn't believe in God, when doubt of God's love and presence held the day for her. She had a simple trust, and somehow, no matter what the situation, she would gain support and strength and comfort from her Savior.

Today, in our sadness and loss, in a time when it appears that death has carried the day, Christ is here, reaching out to strengthen, encourage, and transform our sorrow into joy. For the full life he promises, and life eternal, lie ahead.

As we go on our way today, to our homes, to the classrooms, to the offices, to the places of leisure and play, may we take with us this message, a message that was a life statement for Ruth: "You are where you are so that Christ may be there." "You are where you are so that Christ may be there!" Go in peace. Amen

Art
Age 65

ART LOVED THE OUTDOORS. The outdoors, that grand cathedral of God, was in his blood.

Greater than any building made with hands, the outdoors is where God chooses to meet humans, according to the book of Genesis. It is a sacred place where God communicates with people—in the lush vegetation, in the dark woods, in the clear water, in the bright skies. We are of the earth—formed from earth's dust—so the earth and humans have a bond with one another from the beginning of time. Perhaps that's why the outdoors was in Art's blood.

Art loved the outdoors. Hunting and fishing were part

In the Hollow of God's Hand

of who he was. Being a guide to fishing parties in Wisconsin is no simple job. Of course, you have to have the right equipment, but more important, you have to have a sense of the lake or the river, knowing the deeps and shallows, knowing where the sand bars and weeds are. It involves knowing the best time of day to fish and the kind of lures and bait to use. And all of that depended on what the party was fishing for: walleyes, northerns, bass. Or muskies.

A muskie, now that's a fish. A stubborn fish. A fish that will put up a fight that you better be prepared for. And Art could cast for hours, hoping for a fight with nary a thought of giving up. I doubt if Art got his stubbornness from a muskie, but if you are strong-willed and strong-headed and opinionated, it's got to come from somewhere. I suspect all of you experienced that strong will in many ways.

Maybe it was when you were with him while he worked on a car or truck and he told you in no uncertain terms what the problem was and how it had to be fixed. And he wasn't about to listen to a second opinion or quibble about what it would cost.

Maybe it was when you were hunting or fishing with him and had to deal with his insistence that he knew better than you how long to wait before taking a shot at that buck, or where you'd have the best luck catching the fish you were looking for.

Maybe it was when you observed him tear a motor down on a car or on an appliance for the house and then drive you crazy by not putting it back together.

Maybe it was when you commented that there was no use keeping some outdated auto part, only to have him tell you there was no way he was going to throw it away. He was sure he would use it sometime. And things accumulated and accumulated and accumulated, but you learned it would do no good to argue about it.

I don't know about you, but I never won an argument with my dad, because he insisted he was right, even when he knew he was wrong. That kind of stubbornness can be humorous in retrospect, but it is infuriating at the time.

I've noticed through the years that outdoorsmen often don't appreciate large crowds or being with big groups of people. I understand Art was like that. I suspect he found contentment simply observing nature and thinking. I suspect, too, that his understanding of God came more from that observation than all the years he spent in church. You can't walk in the woods or fish on a lake or sit in a duck blind without making some connection between yourself and nature, without gathering some inkling that there's more to all of this than just a love of the outdoors. Yes, God first met humans in that outdoor cathedral, and that meeting still happens in mysterious and wonderful ways.

In the Hollow of God's Hand

Hank told me, not long before his father's sudden heart attack, that he had asked his dad, "Do you believe in God?" Art responded, "Yes."

Hank, I'm glad you had the guts to ask that question. He needed to respond, not to make you feel good, but for himself. And think about it. This stubborn, strong-headed, close-to-nature man said, "Yes."

When Jenny was on the phone after Art died on Sunday morning, she told someone, "My dad died. He's going to heaven."

God has given that promise to us all. That is why God sent Jesus to this earth and Jesus willingly gave his life to demonstrate love for all creation. And Jesus gave this promise, "I am the resurrection and the life. Those who believe in me, even though they die, will live, and everyone who lives and believes in me will never die."

That's the promise Jesus gives, and this strong-headed, strong-willed Lord of ours never breaks a promise. Thank you, Lord, thank you! Amen

LILA
AGE 69

LISTENING TO THE HYMN "In the Garden" creates a picture in my mind, a picture of Lila in the garden, working with herbs of all sorts. A picture of Lila in the garden alone, privately, quietly planting, appreciating the work, contemplating the beauty and wonder of God's handiwork, wondering what fruit her work will bear. Or maybe looking at the birds that would come to the feeder, listening to their sounds, watching them be nourished by the seed that she or Al had put out for them.

Lila was a private person. She appreciated being alone, appreciated the stillness, the solitude of life.

In the Hollow of God's Hand

During the last few weeks of her life, when she knew she was not going to recover from her breast cancer, she talked about that solitude, about how silence invigorated her. In fact, on more than one occasion, we sat together in silence, reflecting on God's care, reflecting on her condition, rarely breaking the silence. We just sat, enjoying the presence of God—the One who cares for us more fully than for the birds of the air or the lilies of the field. And just enjoying one another's presence, silently, quietly, patiently.

One of Lila's Stephen Ministry friends shared with me how Lila cared deeply for those in need: the people she visited as a Stephen Minister and those who came to donate blood during the blood drive. Maybe that was a sign of the nurse's heart showing through, maybe it was a sign of the care she had come to see God give to the birds of the air and the lilies of the field—and the care God gave to her. Lila's life had not been an easy life, and yet, she had come through, dependent more and more in later years on God who cares for us all.

About two weeks before she died, we sat quietly together for ten minutes or so and talked about Easter. Then we talked about hope when it was pretty clear what all the signs were saying: she would not recover her health, she would not beat the cancer. She had been uncomfortable most of that day, and we spoke of Christ who rose from

In Quietness and Confidence…

the dead, the victorious One, the One who conquered death and pain, sadness and grief. And we prayed for new life and resurrection for all. I held her hands as we prayed words of confidence and faith and hope.

Just a few days ago, Al shared with me some of Lila's writing, and one line stands out. She wrote, "Jesus was in agony before he died, but he rose again." I suspect those words reflected the hope she had for herself as she faced her closing days, knowing her struggle with cancer was almost over.

I have a plaque in my home that says, "In quietness and in confidence shall be your strength." Perhaps in the last weeks of her life, that is what we have seen—not one who was fearful, but one who could trust God for all that would come.

These words from Matthew's sixth chapter are words all of us need to hear: "Therefore I tell you, do not worry about your life, what you will eat or what you will drink, or about your body, what you will wear … Look at the birds of the air; they neither sow nor reap nor gather into barns, and yet your heavenly Father feeds them. Are you not of more value than they? Consider the lilies of the field, how they grow; they neither toil nor spin, yet I tell you, even Solomon in all his glory was not clothed like one of these." Jesus calls us to trust in God's care, to set aside the worry

In the Hollow of God's Hand

that is so destructive to life, to contemplate those birds and the lilies and know that God cares for us, oh so much more.

Al, the promise of Jesus is that God will care for you in this time and in the months that lie ahead. God has promised that. And God never breaks a promise.

And now may the peace of God that passes all understanding be with you always. Amen

DONALD
AGE 70

I REMEMBER HIS QUESTION to this day. It was the night I interviewed with the St. John's congregation. Don had a question that night. My first encounter with him. Not a stumper-type question, just straightforward, honest, direct. His words were something like this: "How often will the two fine young pastors we have here at St. John's be worked into the preaching schedule?" I remember thinking, this man wants me to know something about his convictions with that question. He let me get a little glimpse into him.

Last June, Don and I were eating lunch at Skip's. I reminded him of his question. He smiled, with that coy smile of his, and almost with tongue in cheek he said, "I just wanted to let you know how I felt." Straightforward, honest, direct.

Some minutes later, we talked about his experience at Mayo Clinic when they found the cancer and couldn't operate. "I was scared," he told me, "I was really scared." The words and the tears welling up in his eyes told me something that many men try to hide. But Don didn't. His response was straightforward, honest, direct.

And then I asked, "Don, was God anyplace to be found in that scary, frightening time?" His reply was simple. Tears continuing to well up, he said quietly, "I couldn't have gotten through without him." He talked a bit about the chaplains who visited, about his wife's strong presence, about reading and praying. Straightforward, honest, direct.

Most of you know Don a lot better than I do. You've had the benefit of some years to know him. But in a little over a year, I came to know a man who knew who he was and knew *whose* he was. No wonder he was able to speak with conviction—straightforward, honest, direct.

I could see why, as someone told me, Don was capable of "arousing lots of emotion." Whether you were doing business with him at the bank or serving on the church council with him, whether you were an Air Force buddy or a family member, you knew you were dealing with a man

Straightforward, Honest, Direct

of strong convictions who wasn't afraid to speak them, one who had a sense of right and wrong—straightforward, honest, direct.

He was a man of convictions, one who didn't play favorites. A boss who greeted the janitors and secretaries as openly as those who reported directly to him. A man who treated folks fairly and had a strong sense of fair play. He could disagree strongly, but move on when the vote didn't go his way. Straightforward, honest, direct.

His brother Bob tells of the time he drove with Don from coast to coast. Don loved to drive. But Bob wanted to stop overnight because he couldn't sleep well in the car. Don wasn't much interested. And when Bob awoke, they were already in Nebraska. Don kept on moving, his mind on the destination.

The destination: "Whether we live or whether we die, we are the Lord's." There's comfort in knowing that. There's assurance that enables us to keep moving forward. And when you know that God is with you in death as God has been with you in life, when you are convinced of that, you can move through life confident and be straightforward, honest, direct.

And you can enjoy life: time with family, a game of golf, a walk on the beach, a business meeting, a worship

In the Hollow of God's Hand

service, a conversation, passing on a joke you just heard or enjoying a pun.

You can move through life confident because, as St. Paul assures us, "We are more than conquerors through Christ who loved us. For I am convinced that neither death nor life, nor things present, nor things to come, nor height, nor depth, nor anything else in all creation will be able to separate us from the love of God in Christ Jesus our Lord."

And so today we gather knowing something more about the destination. Knowing death is not the end. For Jesus has promised, though we die, yet we shall live to celebrate with God and all God's people forever.

And holding to God's promise, we can face our life with confidence, held secure in the hollow of God's very hand. Amen

Betty
Age 73

THE CARE OF A MOTHER for her children is a gift of beauty. In just a few weeks we will hear the story of a mother and her son. A story familiar to our ears. A story that pulls at our heart strings. A story of great love.

We will hear of Mary, Jesus' mother. We will imagine her care for her son from the very beginnings of his life. How she nurtured him, protected him, helped him grow, but more important, *let* him grow. We will imagine her support of her son during the time of his work, and finally, we will see her standing near the cross and hear her son speak to her, as he nodded to John, his disciple, to care for his mother: "Woman, here is your son."

In the Hollow of God's Hand

In our faith tradition we sometimes are so focused on the son that we miss the poignancy of this mother's life, this one who is quite possibly the most faithful person ever to have lived.

I mean to draw no direct comparison here, yet I believe it is helpful to reflect on the lives of Mary and her cousin Elizabeth, the mother of John the Baptist, as we grieve this Elizabeth, this Betty, who has influenced your lives and, on one occasion, mine.

As I listened to Betty's sons speak of her love for her sons and her grandchildren, I couldn't help but notice the looks in their eyes, the catches in their throats, the intensity of their feelings. Certainly their relationship with her, like all relationships we have, was filled with flaws, mistakes, difficulty. And yet, it was obvious that something existed between them that we would wish all parents and children could experience and live—a love that encouraged people to treasure one another.

I listened to them speak of their mother's difficult days, of many years alone, of hard work. But I also heard of happy times as Mrs. "Doc" Smith. Of her love of crossword puzzles, where she demonstrated her large vocabulary and familiarity with English learned at the foot of her teacher, Dorothy Hall. Of her delight in being able to beat the *Jeopardy* contestants to the answer. Of her enjoyment in

The Gift of Love

indulging in twice-baked potatoes and a martini (or two) at Christopher's. I heard how she loved desserts and relished laughter and conversation with family and friends. And they told me of her interest in all that her grandkids were doing, of her willingness to take off at the drop of a hat to go for a road trip. Of how she was always there for her sons, and that you'd better not mess with any of Betty's boys or you'd suffer her wrath.

Sure, I know the smoking she did gave her emphysema and probably contributed to the heart attack that caused her death. And I know, like the rest of us, Betty looked back and knew if she had done things differently, if she had taken better care of herself, life might have been different, too.

I held her hand one day in Methodist Hospital. She was not conscious. But she had a presence about her I could sense. The presence of one who had experienced hardship and wouldn't give up. The presence of one who kept on keeping on. I prayed that day, asking God in God's wisdom to bring her through in the way that would be best for her. I thought she probably wouldn't make it, but she did. And she kept on keeping on for a time longer.

Can you see Mary in those verses keeping on keeping on? No easy life, hers, and yet she keeps on going and stands

In the Hollow of God's Hand

close to her son to the very end, loving him every step of the way.

Betty would say to me that I shouldn't get too religious about the comparison, I suppose. And I won't, except to say, Mary was a wise woman, who grasped that love is the most important part of yourself you can give to family.

Mike, Adam, Robert, Steve, and all you grandkids, take that in. Claim that from your mom and grandma. You see, at the heart of our religion is love. Live that for the rest of your days and she'd be most proud of you. And God will smile.

For at the heart of that love is God's deep love for you, offering encouragement and hope for tomorrow, forgiveness and strength for today.

Though she loved Las Vegas, Betty knew life is no crap shoot, it is no wheel of fortune. It is, rather, a gift—a gift of love that God has initiated and we have the privilege of continuing.

I know Betty knew that, because that's what she tried to live and to give—the gift of love that not even death can stop. "For though we die, yet we shall live" to love again. That is the promise of God. Amen

GINNY
AGE 74

TEN DAYS AGO we gathered here. We came to celebrate a life, but we were filled with sadness and loss because Russ had died. Little did we know that we would so soon be with one another again, once more to celebrate a life, but filled once again with sadness and loss, this time because Ginny has died of a heart attack, a heart broken by sadness over her husband's death.

And what can we say? It is difficult, extremely difficult, to go through these kinds of losses, especially when they come one on the heels of another. With the psalmist we may cry out, "How long, O Lord, how long?" Or again,

In the Hollow of God's Hand

"Out of the depths have I cried to you, O Lord. O Lord, hear my voice." Or with Job in his great suffering, we acknowledge, "My spirit is broken." Or maybe with Jesus on the cross we cry out, "My God, my God, why have you forsaken me?"

The burden is heavy today. And as we think of the days and weeks and months ahead when we will be processing these losses, the burden can seem overwhelming. And so it is very important today to hold on to that old slogan that every AA and Al–Anon member has had to cling to in order to keep going, to keep putting one foot in front of the other, to keep moving.

Remember, it's "one day at a time." Today is the only day we can deal with. Today is the only day we have to deal with. So don't dissipate your energy by living in tomorrow, by letting worries or fears about tomorrow dictate what today will be.

Instead, focus on the day. Do the best you can do, be the best you can be. For, as has been so dramatically demonstrated to us, today is all we know we have. There is no way to know how or when we will die. But we know we can focus our energy on the day. We know how to live today. And that's what's important. Today!

And so Ginny lived in the day. Loving and caring, enjoying being a homemaker. Enjoying that golf game or bridge game, or bowling a line when she was physically able

"One Day at a Time"

to do those things. Enjoying the outdoors, enjoying good food and entertaining friends. Enjoying that fellow Russ whom she met on a blind date about fifty-four years ago, and knowing that each day with him would be an adventure. Enjoying the Saturday nights at Al-Anon and the potlucks and the games. Enjoying you.

I was told that Ginny didn't give up easily. That she didn't give in to obstacles. Life was not always easy and family struggles took their toll, but she had a stick-to-it-iveness. She stayed the game, even when things weren't going right.

I suspect not giving up easily comes from living in the day. It comes from not getting out in front of yourself. It comes as you realize all you have to get through is one day, one twenty-four-hour period, one rising and setting of the sun. I have a sneaking suspicion that this is how the psalmist and Job and Jesus all got through: They lived in the day and had strength for the day.

When your hearts are broken, when you think you can't get through, remember the Ginny who didn't give up easily. Let her inspire you.

And let the God Ginny knew be with you in the day. For that is what God wants to do: To be with you. To hear your cries. To comfort your spirit. To share your grief. To renew your hope today so you can keep going and keep putting one foot in front of the other and keep moving.

In the Hollow of God's Hand

"I am with you. I will not leave you or forsake you," God says—that is my promise. I do not cause bad things to happen, nor can I prevent them, but I am with you in them, to share your tears, to keep you going, to give you strength, to renew your life, one day at a time, from here to eternity. Amen

DICK
AGE 75

> Nothing is so strong as gentleness,
> nothing so gentle as real strength.
> *St. Francis de Sales*

THE LIVING OF THESE WORDS is not a task for the fainthearted, and few there may be who are able to embrace it. But sometimes, when we look closely, we discover God has graced our time, our days, with just such a person. And stopping for a moment to reflect, we find we simply want to say, "Thanks." Thanks for the strong gentleness, for the gentle strength.

In the Hollow of God's Hand

It's gentle strength that takes an old broken-down boat, tears it apart and then puts it back together with hard labor and sweat, and takes care to make it shine with a luster none thought possible. It's gentle strength that corrals an ornery church council member and sets him straight in a way that doesn't demean. It's gentle strength that helps encourage a fearful congregation embarking on a building program to claim its possibilities and its ability to pay for the church they want to build. It's gentle strength that knows how to speak the tough word to kids to build them up, and gentle strength that knows, too, when to keep silent.

It's strong gentleness that designs and creates paraments and seasonal inserts for the front of the altar like the one we see today—a design that reflects the mystery of God, the One present and far away, the One pure and holy, the One who is life's beginning and ending and who lives in our midst in Jesus the Christ. It's strong gentleness that envisions a bell tower—never to be built—to hold an old bell so it can announce something of God to a community. It's strong gentleness that gives itself to life. Together with his wife, Dick loved and grew with and brought energy and values and purpose to family and friends.

Gentle strength. Strong gentleness. We beheld it in Dick's character. We observed it in the twinkle of his eye and his sly smile. We heard it in his marvelous, dry sense of

Gentle Strength

humor, in its playfulness and in its bite, too. We saw it as he took his place at worship, as he knelt quietly at the altar, as he held out his hands to receive the bread and wine, as he prayed and as he wept during his long battle with cancer and then Parkinson's disease.

And today, we simply want to say thanks to God for Dick. And Dick would whisper in my ear, "Roy, before you go any further, look at that stained glass picture in the balcony. That Shepherd. Now, there you see it clearly. 'Nothing is so strong as gentleness, so gentle as real strength.'" It isn't that Dick would want to interfere in my sermonizing, though I suspect he was tempted on occasion. But he would want us to get it straight today. God is the important one here.

For life, for times of grief like these and times when joy and wonder can't be contained, it is God, the Shepherd, who is the strong one, the gentle one, the one who lives for us and in us and through us. It is God, the Shepherd, who gives the vision of what we can be today, the courage to move into tomorrow, and the strength to embrace it.

It is the Shepherd who heals our wounds and guides us into green pastures. The Shepherd who walks with us through the valley of the shadow of death and whose promise is good for life on the other side. The Shepherd whom we can count on and who will not disappoint. The

In the Hollow of God's Hand

Shepherd who restores us and brings a smile to the face again, and a twinkle to the eye, and joy to the heart.

Therefore, our thanks today are to God—for what God has already done and what God shall yet do. "Thank you, God."

One day while visiting Dick at Mercy Hospital with some of his family around, I asked him if we should pray. He wasn't too keen on the idea. He thought it would be better to sing the doxology and not to that dull tune in the hymnal, but to the jazz rendition composed by George Paterson, a friend. Well, I stumbled through it once and then had the Lewis Tabernacle Choir members join in. It didn't go very well. So Dick suggested with that twinkle in his eye and just a tinge of sarcasm in his voice that we needed to sing it again.

Maybe it was just his way of saying, "If you're gonna thank and praise God, do it well. Live it well!"

And so we're going to thank and praise God today. And sing the doxology—not according to the tune in the hymnbook, but with jazz. And I have a hunch we'll do it well, with strength and with gentleness, too. And maybe as we do, we'll see in our mind's eye the twinkle in the eye and the smile on the face of Dick, this strong and gentle one, this one who was a friend of God's and of ours. Amen

DON
AGE 75

WE ARE HERE TO CELEBRATE Don's life—a life well lived.

I could sense it as he eagerly responded to my question in the hospital room last Sunday, "Don, would you like to receive communion?" He nodded his head in affirmation. He would share the Lord's Supper that afternoon with his wife, his two daughters, and four of his grandchildren. That small piece of bread soaked in a bit of wine. "The body and blood of Christ given and shed for you," I said. There was a tear in his eye as he surveyed the room where the others waited to share in the meal.

You get a sense of the true person in a hospital room

when he knows he doesn't have many more sunrises to see. I looked at Don and there was no fear in his eyes. Death would not be his master. He had another one!

I can only imagine how many worship services he sat through in his fifty-one years at St. John's. How many sermons heard. How many trips to the communion rail to receive that presence of the living One, that assurance that Jesus' love knows no bounds. And when that gets through to you, life is different. It can be enjoyed in fresh ways. It can be well lived.

Don built those intricate model ships, and you can see them around the house where he and Mary Jane lived. I can't imagine how much work, how much patience, how much skill, how much care it must have taken to make ships like that—so well built.

A ship is a symbol for the Christian church—the ship that keeps us safe as we travel over the troubled waters of life. The ship that gets us through life's storms. The ship that carries us through a well-lived life, because the ship's captain, Jesus Christ, is the one who navigates the ship through storm and trouble to calm and safety.

Don knew the captain, the same captain who came to his disciples in their storm-tossed boat two thousand years ago and spoke words of comfort and reassurance: "It is I. Do not be afraid." And that, I would say, is the very reason Don's life was well lived.

A Life Well Lived

Some of you knew Don as an avid golfer, one who would play five days a week when possible and enjoy every moment. One who loved the golf stories that go with the game. And one who didn't surrender to using a golf cart until this past year.

Some of you knew Don as one who loved music and who played the baritone in three different bands and loved the music that is so much a part of St. John's.

Some of you knew him as a man proud of his country, who served with honor as a paratrooper with the 82nd Airborne Division in World War II and received the Purple Heart.

Some of you knew Don as that dedicated fan who loved sports of most every kind, who played avidly back at East High, and loved to cheer on teams and individual sports contestants, too.

Some of you knew him as a fellow who just loved to have fun and share humor, who had an easy way about him and took life in stride.

And many of you knew Don as the kind of friend worth having, a guy with integrity and good judgment, a fellow who knew everybody on the job in those days at Iowa Power and Light.

A few years ago he lost sight in one eye but kept right on playing golf and still managed to master the computer.

In the Hollow of God's Hand

We're here to celebrate Don's life—a life well lived. A life grounded in a God who loved him and in a Savior who promised, "I am the resurrection and the life." A life lived on a ship called the church that helped him navigate all his days.

This same God, this same Savior, and this same ship are present today to comfort and carry you—Mary Jane and family and friends—through these troubled times of grieving and loss.

May God use us to embrace our friends with love and care, and to speak Jesus' promise to them: "I am the resurrection and the life." On that promise we can count. Amen

Carroll
Age 76

I'll always remember his large hands. Carroll and Lilah would sit near the end of that second pew on the lectern side of the church. I could count on them to be there when they weren't snowbirding down at Apache Junction, Arizona. Sunday after Sunday, they would be there, singing, listening, praying.

And then they would come to the table to receive communion—with common cup. And I'll always remember Carroll's large hands taking that small piece of bread and then wrapping around the chalice—holding it fast as he drank.

In the Hollow of God's Hand

Those large hands served Carroll well. Through those many years of farming—of working the land, of fixing machinery. Those times of loading livestock on and off the truck that he drove years ago. Those twenty-five years of handling packages and letters for the post office.

I can see those hands at work now restoring that 1935 John Deere B tractor. It had been his father's first tractor, steel wheels and all. And then it became Carroll's pride and joy, and he'd shine it up after anybody had touched it and would start it now and then, remembering, I suspect, the early days, the times he drove it as a kid, his hands wrapped firmly around the wheel.

I can see those hands at work helping to build the Zion Parish Hall and Educational Unit back in the fifties, or again in the sixties, stoking the heat pots in the new sanctuary during winter nights so that construction could continue day after day.

I can see those hands at work, packing the car, hitching up the trailer, setting up camp, catching and cleaning fish, as, year after year, he took his family on summer trips, making their way to most every state in the union.

In so many ways Carroll was a hands-on kind of fellow. Never afraid of hard work. Always ready to serve, here at Zion on the church council for twenty years, with the Zion

Strong Hands

Home Builders group, or working with Lilah as adviser to the Luther League long ago, or ringing the bell.

But, most of all, I can see those hands wrapped around a cup of coffee or hugging a child, holding a grandkid or holding a pinochle hand as he sat at his favorite place—not a soft chair in the living room, but at the kitchen table, happiest when the kids were all there, taking in the blessings of the day.

You know, so much of life happens at table, here in church and in our homes—we eat there of course, but we converse there, too, or we just sit and ponder, maybe spend some moments in thankfulness for all we've been given.

I wonder, today, how many times this quiet man, this good man, this trusting man must have looked at those hands and then folded them in prayer and thanked God for it all. My guess is that it happened often.

Today, we gather to hear the promises of a God whose hands are so strong that the whole world is in them. Today, wounded and weary by the loss of Carroll to a stroke, we discover the hands of God, supporting us, giving us strength, helping us to go on.

Those hands reached out to touch the brokenhearted, to heal the infirm, to give hope to those who had lost hope. And today, we are invited to put our hand in the hand of

In the Hollow of God's Hand

the Shepherd who leads us through the valley of the shadow of death and promises that all who put their hand in his shall dwell in the house of the Lord forever. Thanks be to God. Amen

JAMES
AGE 76

HOW MANY HERE ever heard Jim tell a joke? Raise your hand. How many ever shared a joke with Jim? And how many had a real strong inkling that Jim planned his jokes and planned exactly when he was going to tell them?

In talking with the family the other day, I got the feeling that Jim had as much fun telling jokes as folks did hearing them, even if they were sometimes groaners. In fact, maybe that was even half the fun. And many of you are going to remember all that fun as you think of Jim, because fun and enjoyment and appreciation of life and family and friends and work and learning and service were all part of the Jim who touched you. And he planned everything.

In the Hollow of God's Hand

For he was a planner, par excellence, whether he was planning as an architect, planning as a cook, planning as a pilot, planning as a speaker, or planning when he might tell certain jokes and to whom.

"In my Father's house are many rooms," John's Gospel tells us. Rooms that are well designed, rooms to accommodate people, to enable functions, to appeal to the aesthetic senses. For between forty and fifty years, Jim planned Dahl's stores and the remodeled Longfellow School and the East and West Side Branch Libraries and so many other places, commercial and residential. In his offices downtown, he planned, he created, he worked with contractors and builders and business leaders. In the Des Moines Register there was an ad for the sale of a house. At the end of the description it said, "Jim Lynch, architect—quality."

I couldn't resist reading from Isaiah today. It seemed made for this occasion, as we celebrate the life of a connoisseur of fine wine and a gourmet cook and one who appreciated well-prepared food. Listen again. "On this mountain the Lord of hosts will make for all peoples a feast of fat things, a feast of wine on the lees, of fat things full of marrow, of wine on the lees well refined."

In the Twenty-third Psalm we read, "Thou preparest a table before me." Jim knew that a gracious table doesn't just happen. It takes planning. It takes work. One can see

The Plans I Have for You

him poring over his almost two hundred cookbooks searching for just the right recipes, inviting his guests to "come and see" in the kitchen, to behold the bird at Thanksgiving or whet their appetites by savoring the sights and smells of the dinner about to be served. One can see him choosing the right wine, though not always the most expensive. He planned. Many of you enjoyed. The food, the wine, the conversation, the jokes, the time around the table.

We may be more conscious of our diets and fat intake today, but I think the Lord has a soft spot for those who appreciate good food and fine wine, and who meticulously plan with time and effort to serve the very best.

There are no texts in the Bible about flying, though I remember the story of the Sunday School kid who said, "There must have been airplanes in Jesus' time because it does talk about Pontius the pilot." (A groaner? Yes, but I think Jim might have liked it.) And we all know if you're going to fly, you need to have a flight plan, in detail, to make sure you know where you are going and when and how you can go there in the safest way possible, given all the other flights that are planned.

Jim got his first taste of flying in a biplane when he was eight years old. And it got into his blood. He loved flying, as a pilot in the military and in his own Cessna 182. And he loved to do the March of Dimes flights, giving little kids an opportunity to get in a plane, too.

In the Hollow of God's Hand

Yes, Jim planned, and he planned well. Doug said you could ask him the time and he would tell you how to build a watch. He was given to detail, to learning, to knowing, to reading, to sharing, to caring—and his life was planned well.

In Jeremiah 29:11, we read, "'For surely I know the plans I have for you,' says the Lord, 'plans for your welfare and not for harm, to give you a future with hope.'" God was speaking to the Israelites living in exile in Babylon. God speaks of their deliverance from bondage and their return home to the Promised Land.

God's plans for us are always for good, that we might live fully and nobly, delighting in life and blessing the lives of family and friends and the communities where we live.

To that end, God promises to journey with us all our days. To that end, God promises to walk with us into death, as God walked with Jim when he suffered a sudden blood clot before surgery. And to that end, God sent Jesus Christ to be one of us, to help us see what God is really like, to help us know God loves and cares for us always.

You see, God's plan is "to give you a future with hope," and God knows resurrection and new life don't just happen, so God planned it. And Jesus says to us all, "Come and see." "Come and see." "I am the resurrection and the life." "Because I live, you will live also." Now, that's a plan worth knowing, and a planner worth trusting. Amen

LEONARD
AGE 79

YOU COULD SEE IT in his eyes. A love of life. A love of people. A love of God. A love of work. It was that twinkle, that look of delight. It could calm a crying child and soothe a mother's concern and affirm adolescent boys and girls. "My father chose pediatrics," son Mark said, "so he could care for and nurture new life." And that's what he did. More than thirty-eight years as a pediatrician enabled "Dr. G" to touch the lives of countless families. There were the unending house calls, a practice not followed so faithfully today. There were hours consoling a mother who feared for her child's life. There was the time invested in young

In the Hollow of God's Hand

men and women, giving them encouragement all along the way. And the many occasions when a patient's bill was simply marked "Paid by Dr. G," when he knew the patient couldn't afford to pay for the office call or the treatment given.

There was the time Dr. G served as a cabbie, taking a patient who had fainted in the office home when the patient was feeling better. There were the innumerable times he relaxed kids who were to get a shot by putting a butter cookie with the hole in the center over the hypodermic needle. There was the advice given to a young father. "Boil the nipples," Dr. G told him, thinking they were both talking about bottle nipples. Well, you can fill in the rest of the story. There was a love of life. A love of people. A love of work.

"Someday I should write a book," he could be heard saying on one of those days when he had been with countless patients. And write a book he did, not with paper and pen, but a book writ large in the lives of people, in the care he took for them, in the wisdom he offered them, in the encouragement he gave them, in the laughter he shared with them, in the spark of life he enjoyed with them.

Words like "generous, kind, patient" are used by many who have shared life with Len through the years. I'd like to use the word "faithful." He was a faithful man. Some time ago, Len wrote about four people who had influenced his life in extremely significant ways: his mother, the principal of his high school, the dean of the medical school he attended, and, most of all, his wife.

In the way he lived his life—in his eagerness to learn, in his dedication to working hard, in his commitment to values that make a difference in the world, in his love for the woman he met when she was in college and whom he married some fifty years ago—Len was a man of deep faithfulness. A faithfulness learned early in church in northern Minnesota, I suspect. A faithfulness practiced through worship and concern for the health ministry of this congregation. A faithfulness practiced as he stood humbly before God and as he walked humbly with others, always showing dignity and respect for all God's creation.

A faithfulness that was sorely tested by the deaths of two of his sons and then tested again during the last six years of his life as his body wasted away from the effects of systemic sclerosis, an autoimmune disease that went undiagnosed for three of those years.

But through it all, he understood the faithfulness of God. A faithful God who cares for all of life. A faithful God who consents to become one with the human family to encourage us and love us and strengthen us and give us hope. Today this faithful God is present, mourning, too, the death of a friend. Mourning, too, with family and friends

In the Hollow of God's Hand

and telling us, "Come to me all who labor and are heavy laden and I will give you rest." And promising, "Though we die, yet we shall live." And promising to be with us every step of the way. And promising, "I am with you always." And promising, "Not even death can separate us from the love of God."

This God, too, has written a book. It, too, is a book writ large upon the lives of those, like Len, who have come to know God, to trust God, to let themselves be loved by God, to risk walking with God, to share the divine spark that God has given, and to let it be seen by all who cross their path. That is the kind of life and relationship with God that Mother Teresa described when she said, "I feel like a pencil in God's hand. God writes through us—and however imperfect instruments we may be—God writes beautifully."

Indeed, our faithful God wrote beautifully through Len's life and will continue to write through ours, now and into eternity. Amen

DONALD
AGE 79

IT WAS ON ONE of those visits with Don in the hospital, one day a couple of years ago, that I thanked him. As a relatively new pastor here at St. John's, I had become aware of the strokes Don had had, of Don's battle with cancer, of his fight to live, of his positive attitude, of his openness to God's leading. "Don," I said, "thank you for being a witness to me every time we are together."

During those visits, I was supposed to be the one ministering to him, and yet I left feeling that I had been ministered to by Don. I would leave his hospital room feeling better than when I had entered, simply because I had been with him, enjoying a story, sharing a laugh, engaging in a serious conversation, offering a prayer.

Early on, I learned from others that Don had been instrumental in the Door of Faith Mission. And I recall a member of the board of the Churches United Shelter sharing how committed Don was to that ministry and to the homeless of this community, how willing he was to share himself and his leadership abilities with that most important venture. I can understand how the people served in those places would feel better, too, because of Don's commitment to care and justice, especially for those who were the most needy in our community.

The other night, someone in the family said, "Don always had a smile, even when things weren't going well for him, even when his illness these past years was most critical."

I suspect he smiled because a smile is always a gift to others, and Don had discovered along the way of life that giving was what life was all about. That giving was the joy of life. It was the only way to live, if one wanted to live to the full.

Jesus tells us that he loves us for a reason: "So that my joy may be in you, and that your joy may be complete." Some folks in life don't seem to get that. But Don caught on. And all of us—family and friends, Air Corps buddies from long ago and business associates and colleagues from

A Giving Life

more recently, folks in his neighborhood, folks in the shelter for the homeless, and folks in the larger community where he provided leadership—have been beneficiaries of that joy that was his.

In our memory, joy can still be seen in his broad smile as the wind fills the sails with Don at the helm of the boat. Seen when he shows friends the myriads of photographs taken as he traveled the world. Seen in that wry look he has when he taunts his good Republican friends by wearing a "Vote Democrat" tie. Seen in his cheerful face as he sits in a chair surrounded by those he loves. Seen in his tear-filled eyes as he says, "Amen," to conclude the prayer we share together.

When we know the good news of God for us and take it in, we discover a zest for living, a joy in life, a reason for giving. We discover life as Jesus meant it for us all so that our "joy may be complete."

In these past days, joy has not been easy to find. But in our time of sadness and loss, we sense its presence is near as we hear Jesus' words: "I have loved you… so that my joy may be in you, and that your joy may be complete." We catch it in the powerful words from the book of Isaiah where God says, "Do not fear, for I am with you, do not be afraid, for I am your God; I will strengthen you, I will help you, I will uphold you with my victorious right hand."

In the Hollow of God's Hand

Even today, the sound of victory can be heard. Jesus says, "I am the resurrection and the life. Because I live, you will live also." Here. Today. And forever. Now, let "my joy be in you, that your joy may be complete."

Thank you, Lord, for letting us savor the pleasure of Don's company as he witnessed to us of your joy. And let your joy be in us all the rest of our days. Amen

GEORGE
AGE 80

I SUSPECT GEORGE is delighted to have his memorial service held on this day, amid all the signs of Easter, amid the sea of lilies reminding us of the most important festival of the Christian community, amid the arrangements of daffodils and spring flowers that speak of new life, amid a sanctuary that focuses on the risen Christ.

I can almost see that smile on his face and the twinkle in his eye, because everywhere we look in this place the focus is on Jesus, the risen One, the One who gives us hope, the One who knew George and whom George knew.

Over fifty years ago now, a young man was serving his

In the Hollow of God's Hand

country in the Pacific fleet of the U.S. Navy. It was toward the end of the war. The LST 396 on which George served was hit and sank in the South Pacific. And through that night, George and others found themselves in a raft adrift in the dark—not knowing where they were, not knowing what their fate would be when the sun arose the next morning, not knowing if they would ever be rescued.

I would not pretend to know what George, along with those other Navy men, experienced that night—fear, anger, sadness, emptiness, longing, grief, despair. I don't know if he prayed or how he prayed, but something is quite clear to me. Perhaps then, perhaps later, but at some point in his life, George chose not to live his years adrift. He would live them moored, anchored, secured to that which gave hope.

The Gospel text for today tells of followers of Jesus who were soon to be adrift in the world. Jesus was returning to the Father, and what were they to hold on to? How would they keep going?

They would not be able to ask him for guidance anymore as they walked the dusty roads of Palestine. They would not be able to engage him in conversation across the table about the questions they had. He was leaving them. Plain and simple.

And so, Jesus reached out to them with words of promise and hope. "I go to prepare a place for you ... I will

From Adrift to Moored

come again and take you to myself … I am the way, the truth, and the life."

In these brief verses, Jesus addresses all of us who find ourselves adrift in life. He calls us to step forth and to follow him—the way, the truth, the life. He calls us to step forth and to trust that he is a person of his word, that he can be trusted, that his promises are true, and that in him there is a full and abundant life. Even in the face of George's unexpected death from a stroke, Jesus calls us to trust that life and joy can be restored.

I understand that George loved sailing. So he knew not only about sailing, but also about making sure his boat was moored, was anchored, was secured, so it would not go adrift at the end of the day.

And he knew about the importance of mooring his own life, too. Maybe that is what we were really seeing as he set sail confidently across the lake or as he welcomed us so hospitably with his smile and the twinkle in his eye. Maybe that is what we were really seeing as he glided with ease across the dance floor or as he lived his devotion to Betsy and family. Maybe that is what we were really seeing as he engaged eagerly with the young and was so ready to have fun. Maybe that is what we were seeing as he crossed the threshold of this place so joyfully and reached out his hand to receive bread and wine so humbly. Maybe that is what

In the Hollow of God's Hand

we were seeing as this gentleman and gentle spirit, anchored in Jesus, touched our spirits.

People who are adrift in life don't evidence confidence and openness, devotion and serving, joy and humility. But people who are anchored, who are secured, who are moored to what gives real life, do.

It started to happen for the disciples when the Spirit came into their lives, when they discovered that the Lord who had left them was still with them. It continued as the truth of Jesus risen took hold of them, and they began to live confidently and devotedly and became servants with joy and humility. They were no longer adrift, but anchored in Jesus, the resurrection and the life.

And so we have come to this place! On Easter Eve! The sanctuary, filled with signs of Easter, with professions of resurrection, fills us with hope. For because we are anchored to this Jesus, whom God raised from the dead, we know his resurrection is no idle tale, nor will ours be. It is the word and promise of God. Thanks be to God. Amen

Lester
Age 80

IF JESUS WERE AROUND in our time and looking for disciples, I think he would have found a way to convince a strong-willed, somewhat gruff but lovable fellow named Lester to follow him. You see, Jesus took a liking to folks who liked to fish. And Lester loved to fish. You might remember Peter, James, and John, those three strong-willed, hard-working fishermen Jesus called to follow him centuries ago.

Sometimes I wonder about the bond that Jesus had with folks who liked to sit around and fish. Was it because they had the patience to wait, and wait, and wait? Patience is a real virtue if you're gonna be a fisherman. You better

In the Hollow of God's Hand

have it, 'cause fish have a mind of their own and don't bite according to the fisherman's schedule. And you sure need patience, too, for the living of life, which doesn't always move according to our schedule. Life takes its own time, and sometimes things come our way—tough things, hurtful things, sad things—things that take time to work through. And patience comes in handy.

Or did Jesus notice that those same folks who liked to fish were also folks who could get excited when a fish took the bait? How fast they were able to move then—setting the hook, reeling in the line. Broad smiles and then the shouting and laughter.

If you were with Lester in the summer up in Canada or in the winter on the Texas coast or at one of the streams not too far from Whittier, you probably experienced some of that patience. Maybe some of that excitement, too.

Maybe you saw that excitement in him when he played high school football. Maybe you caught a bit of it as you watched him watch his grandkids in their sporting events. Maybe you were witness to it when he finished up some of those toy boxes for the grandchildren. Maybe you observed it while playing a game of five hundred or pinochle. Or you just picked it up through the years as Lester waited on you in the grocery store or took care of you at the locker plant

The Patience of a Fisherman

or saw to it that you got your mail when he served at the Whittier Post Office.

You know, excitement isn't always noisy. Sometimes it's quiet—more like Lester's was. And yet, you can see it when a man is giving you the best service he can give, sense it when he's industrious and honest, feel it when you know he loves you and cares for you and is grateful for the joy you've brought to his days. Excitement takes all kinds of shapes.

And so does patience. Lester's patience came in handy dealing with the public from behind a grocery store counter or the counter of a post office or driving busloads of kids day after day. Patience isn't easy to learn, but once you've learned it, it serves you well.

Patience serves you well when illness strikes and when the going gets tough and when health begins to wane and when the body doesn't work like it once did and you are a big, independent, stubborn fellow who can't care for the lawn that you always took so much pride in or do the repairs or remodeling around the house that you loved to do.

Lester found that out during these past months battling cancer. It was a struggle when the world had to be observed from inside the house, from his own chair, and then from his bed. His world got smaller as his body wasted away.

In the Hollow of God's Hand

And the patience learned by a man who liked to fish helped him through.

Today, we come together—sad because of our loss, but just plain happy that a fellow like Lester crossed our paths, entered our lives, shared some of his patience, some of his excitement, some of his quietness, some of his love, some of his faith, some of his understanding that God is a patient God, a loving God, a God who is with you as you cast your line and wait.

I started by saying that if Jesus were around in our time I think he would have called a fellow named Lester to follow him. Well, Jesus did. And Lester learned what it meant to follow. Not any more perfectly than the rest of us. Probably not any less perfectly either. But faithfully—living and serving people with integrity, struggling through difficult times, learning to be patient, finding ways to provide you, in his own quiet fashion, some love along the way.

Today, this Jesus whom Lester followed, comes to us to hold us, befriend us, and affirm for us the promise of eternal life. You see, today isn't the end of Lester's story, nor ours. There's more to come, a lot more, when we know whom to follow. Amen

*P*AT
AGE 83

FOR EVERYTHING THERE IS A SEASON and a time for every matter under heaven: a time for golf and a time to refrain from golfing, a time to catch fish and a time to tell stories about the ones that got away, a time to travel and a time to stay home, a time to take control and a time to really take control, a time to care and a time to care some more.

I know this is an extremely loose translation of the biblical text, but think about it when you think about this fellow, Pat, who loved God and loved those whom God surrounded him with. Here's a guy who understood that life lived to the full is life touched by the joy of birth and

In the Hollow of God's Hand

the sadness of death, by planting time and harvest, by weeping and laughing, by mourning and dancing.

There is something you can see in the eyes of someone who enjoys life. That's what I remember seeing the first summer Saturday service he attended after I arrived at St. John's. I suspect that Pat and Bev's habit of coming to Saturday service may have had something to do with a tee time on Sunday, though I could be wrong. He had that look in his eye, an impish look, the kind of look that told me this guy was full of stories—people stories, stories to make you laugh and stories that spoke of caring, stories that told you life is worth living.

I asked family members to reminisce a bit about Pat. I thank all of you who shared. I was amazed by what you wrote, about your total delight with him, about how much fun he was. There were stories about the handkerchief mouse, the nonsense songs, the nose honking and pulling coins from kid's ears, and the hours spent reading stories to kids and letting them comb his "hair." There was the care he showed for family and friends alike, the special thoughtfulness he had for everyone from sister "Boots" to you, when he affirmed you for all your little and big successes. There was the example he set for all by living his beliefs so all of you could see them. He trusted you would do the same.

For Everything a Season

Some of you knew Pat as family, some as military buddy, some as academic colleague, some as fellow engineer, some as faithful church member.

God knew him as friend. God cared for him and he cared for God. Pat understood life's rhythms, life's seasons, where birth and death are part of a full life, and weeping and laughter walk hand in hand, and mourning and dancing embrace.

Skip mentioned how hard it was to play a round of golf with Pat and Bev because they stopped so often during their game to talk with friends. Think on that. In the long run, it's friendship that makes for life. It's friendship that makes life full. It's friendship that puts you in touch with what is most important about living. We are created to live together, to savor life together, to share ourselves and who we are together, to experience life's ups and downs together.

It's part of God's plan. And Pat caught on. And you have experienced a funny, caring, loving, talented, intelligent, faithful, wise friend. You loved a man with a big heart, whose heart suddenly gave out. And today, you're not laughing, you're not dancing. You're sad. And rightly so.

God's arms embrace you in your sadness. And God says, Don't forget how to laugh, don't forget how to dance. For you will do so again.

Tomorrow is Good Friday, and we will reflect again on

In the Hollow of God's Hand

Jesus' death. But on Sunday we will celebrate again Jesus' resurrection. We'll put on our dancing shoes and kick up our heels and sing, "I will sing unto the Lord for he has triumphed gloriously. The grave is empty, won't you come and see."

Today is like Good Friday for you. And as Tony Campolo said in his Good Friday sermon some years ago, "It's Friday now—but Sunday's a-comin'!"

For all the world, it's Friday now. For you, it's Friday now. For all those who grieve, it's Friday now. But the promise of God in Jesus is this: "Sunday's a-comin'!" "Sunday's a-comin'!" "Sunday's a-comin'!" Thanks be to God! Amen

GEORGE
AGE 83

GEORGE WAS JUST plain fun to be with. Whether he was with you in a boat waiting for the fish to bite, or selling popcorn with Kiwanis buddies in the old downtown, or ringing the Salvation Army bell at Christmas, or picking up litter along the highway, or sitting at the house sipping a bit of Lambrusco with friends, or kibitzing around the table in Weertz Hall after service on Sunday.

George was just fun to be with. His smile, his easy way, his teasing, his humor. Well, you just enjoyed being with George.

And whether you were family or friends, there was

In the Hollow of God's Hand

usually much wisdom to be gained by being with him. His knowledge was broad, his tips were practical, his heart was good.

I've chosen the two passages from Proverbs that speak about wisdom, because they fit him. "Wisdom is with the humble," Proverbs 11:2, and "Those who walk in wisdom come through safely," Proverbs 28:26.

George thought clearly, deeply, generously, compassionately. The family was telling me the other day, as they began preparing for this service, that more than once someone said, "We've got to ask Dad." I suspect that will happen often in the months ahead.

George knew a lot. As a builder he knew how to design a plan for a house. He knew how to put it all together. He knew how to run his business well. But he had more than knowledge. He was also wise. He was alert to how you treat people, sensitive to how you work with them, respectful in how you listen to them. No wonder one of his and Betty's neighbors said to me, "George was the best house builder around and everybody knew it," because he took time to get it right, to know what the buyer wanted. And he put a bit of love in each place he built because it reflected something of what was in him.

Wisdom walks with humility in life. They go together. We've all known people who thought they were wise, but

Those Who Walk in Wisdom

their arrogance told us another story. George was very different that way. Somehow he understood that life is meant not for self-aggrandizement, but for being with and caring for those around you.

How many of his neighbors weren't the beneficiaries of his help with their home projects? How many sitting here today didn't discover that George always had time for you, that he never said, "No," even when he should have? How many haven't been touched by his generous giving of time and self?

That has to do with humility. That has to do with knowing we are in this world not simply for our own sake but for the sake of others. And then to do what we do well, with a passion that benefits others, whether it is building a solid house, or sharing a piece of woodworking, or taking time to help a neighbor with a garage door that won't close or a leaky faucet that keeps dripping, or sharing some wisdom with someone who has a problem and needs you to listen and give advice or encouragement.

Wisdom has to do with knowing how to be humble. It's one of the marks of faithful living—living humbly before God and all the people with whom we share life's stage.

Sunday after Sunday, George and Betty sat in the west transept, worshiping together. Sunday after Sunday they

In the Hollow of God's Hand

opened their hands to receive bread and wine. Sunday after Sunday they prayed. There's a certain wisdom that brings folks to do that. And "those who walk in wisdom come through safely."

So when the tough family times came, they came through safely. And when the difficult times struggling with prostate cancer came, they came through safely. Then came the stroke that took George from us. And now, God promises that you will come through safely, even walking through the "valley of the shadow of death." For those who walk in wisdom, those who walk in Christ, come through safely, because the Christ who came to be one with us, died and rose again for us and says, "I am the resurrection and the life." "Though you die, yet shall you live." "Because I live, you will live also."

George entered death's door safely. And so will you. That is our confidence on this day! God is our wisdom, our hope, our victory. "Thanks be to God who gives us the victory through our Lord Jesus Christ." Amen

Ruth
Age 84

RUTH, A SMALL, FRAIL WOMAN, was, in some ways, larger than life. In a day when faithfulness is sometimes ridiculed and people are supposed to be into life for themselves, Ruth lived a faithfulness that witnesses to what life can be.

For years, that faithfulness was demonstrated by her dedication to and companionship with her mother, Catherine. Following the early death of her father, daughter and mother became fast friends, and that faithfulness lasted for decades until her mother's passing.

But there was more faithfulness. Ruth also kept in close touch with the rest of the family—with her sister Virginia and Virginia's children. Ruth was faithful to her job as a tax examiner for the IRS, carrying out her job with the efficiency and care that such a position demands, and also, long after her retirement, maintaining relationships and friendships with coworkers.

Some of you know of her faithfulness to her dachshund, Susie, from whom she was inseparable. Some of you know of her faithfulness to her Danish heritage and the pride she took in letting folks know she was a Dane.

Some of you know of her faithfulness to her church and how she would arrive early in order to get that parking spot nearest the north side ramp. And that as long as she could get out, she never missed worship at St. John's. When that was no longer possible, she always worshiped with the people of St. John's by way of the radio broadcast.

One might easily be discouraged by one's disabilities. And yet Ruth wasn't. With an amputated leg, scoliosis of the spine, and significant lung problems, Ruth might well have given up, but that wasn't her. Her sense of pride in who she was and her independence give us all a model of how one can live strongly and fully even with major physical disability.

My sense of Ruth, from all that you, her family and friends, have told me, is that her gift of faithfulness came from knowing a faithful God as her companion through

A Faithful Life. A Faithful God

life. A God whose love encouraged her, whose forgiveness comforted her, whose guidance directed her, whose truth inspired her, whose presence assured her and brought her serenity and peace.

Through difficult times and times of joy, her God was her companion. And today I say to you, her sister and her nieces and nephew and friends, God is also *your* companion. For God promises, "I am with you." "I will not leave you or forsake you."

As we support one another in our grief, we are reminded of the promise of God that Jesus is the resurrection and the life, and that though we die, yet we shall live. Those promises can be trusted. For God is faithful, above all, and never breaks a promise.

Is that what drew Ruth to church every week and to the radio when she could no longer get there? Those who knew her best were convinced it was. God's faithfulness is the heart of the Gospel, the good news for all, especially when we walk through the valley of the shadow of death.

And for today and tomorrow, that is what our faithful friend Ruth would have us know: God is faithful. God is our companion. God is with us. And that offers us real hope. Thanks be to God. Amen

Maybelle
Age 86

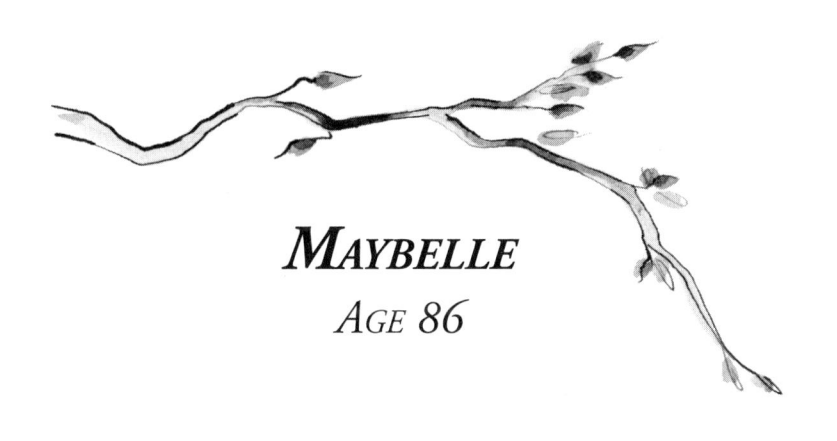

> All flesh is like grass,
> and all its glory like the flower of grass.
> The grass withers, and the flower fades,
> but the word of the Lord endures forever.
> *I Peter 1:24-25a*

THE KITCHEN IS SMALL on College Court. I drank lots of coffee through the years at the table looking over the back yard. Back in the early eighties, Ed would make the coffee. Later, it would be Maybelle who did the honors. A few times, I even made the coffee myself in that kitchen and got some ice cream out of the freezer and scooped it up. Maybelle didn't have much strength at those times. And we'd sit and talk and sometimes just look out at the flowers growing and blossoming in the yard and be quiet.

Maybelle was good at being quiet. Sometimes I'd ask her where she was as she looked out that window, and she'd take a long time responding and then she would tell me about a special time with Ed or family or friends or work that she remembered. And she'd smile that coy smile of hers that always lit up the moment.

And then we'd share bread and wine and let the story of God and God's love and passion for the creation and for us human beings refresh and renew us. And it was good.

The flower grows and blossoms. Like Maybelle. How she loved her life of nursing. How good she was at it. How passionate she was about it as she worked with children at the convalescent home and then with the students at the infirmary. "I'd rather work than go to a party," she'd say. And it was good.

The flower grows and blossoms. With family and friends. Ah, the gatherings that were so important. And the bridge games. The creak of the card table legs was the sure sign that an afternoon bridge party was at hand with the girls—Elsi and Naomi and Jane and Doris and Marce and Minnie and Dorothy and how many more through the

Flowers Blossom and Fade

years. That was fun for Maybelle, exciting. She was passionate about it and about the friends she came to care so deeply about through the years.

The flower grows and blossoms. As she helped friends and family and patients and neighbors, I wonder if Maybelle didn't see the lives of others as flowers to be cared for, nourished, nurtured. How did she care for you? Can you remember the kindnesses, the help, the guidance? Joyce shared a story of some thirty-six years ago, shortly after Tim was born. Joyce, worn out as most new mothers tend to be, looked out the window that day. And there was Maybelle, getting out of the back of a Yellow Checker cab, her upright Hoover vacuum cleaner in hand, ready to go to work, to help out, to make life a little easier for one she loved.

The flower grows and blossoms. And then begins to fade. The last years of her life. Her final weeks at home. And then her last days at Crestview Nursing Home in West Branch. Finally, a few days ago, the flower peacefully died. Her beauty and grace have been seen and remembered. And in the remembering, other lives are nourished for growing and blossoming, too. "The grass withers, and the flower fades, but the word of the Lord endures forever." And the word of the Lord for Maybelle and for us this day

In the Hollow of God's Hand

is "I am the resurrection and the life. Because I live, you also will live!"

Some years ago, a young boy rode his bike to the florist to buy a rose and a small rose bowl for his grandmother. She loved roses. Over the sidewalks he rode for some two miles, up and down at each curb, carefully holding on to his surprise. And then, with delight in his eyes, he presented the rose to Grandma Maybelle at her home.

In honor of Maybelle, in tribute to her, roses are being brought to the table this morning by grandchildren. Can you see the gladness in her eyes? And can you hear her encouragement for how you can live the rest of your days? Blossom and grow! Blossom and grow!

It's what God intends for all of us. Let us delight God by doing just that. Amen

DOROTHY
AGE 86

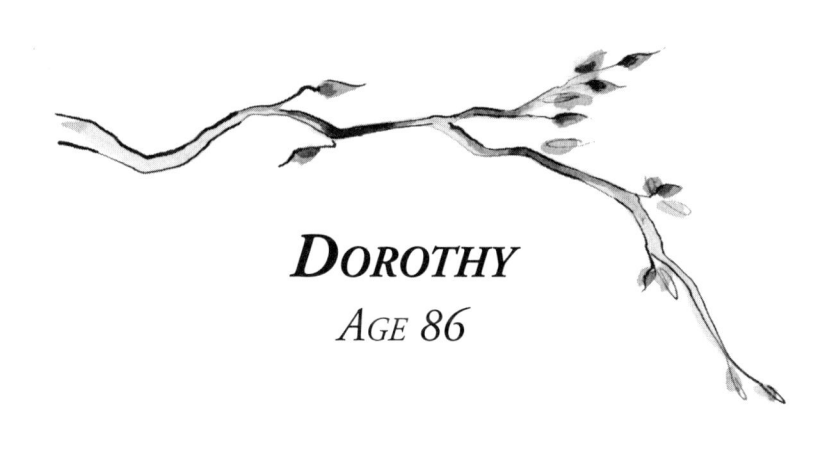

FOR DOROTHY, the world was a big, grand, wonderful place. A place to explore. A place to grow. A place to see how God was at work beyond the little town of Scotland, South Dakota, beyond the Des Moines community, beyond the world of teaching or the blood bank at Mercy Hospital. Dorothy defined the world, not by the safe and the familiar, but by the challenging and the unfamiliar.

She and her friend Darlene traveled far and wide in their eighteen trips together, from South America to the Far East, from Scandinavia to Africa. All in all, Dorothy visited seventy-one countries on five continents and learned

In the Hollow of God's Hand

and appreciated and grew. During a time when some Iowans were fearful of people of other cultures and of other religions, Dorothy visited those folks on their own turf, in their own communities, in their own countries, and grew to appreciate their struggles, their hopes, their dreams, their possibilities, their friendships. And she thought Iowa would be a grand place for many of them to come and live.

Dorothy shared the stories of the peoples and the places she visited. If you ever saw one of her travelogues, you were treated, not only to fine photography, but also to thoughtful commentary with a sense of humility and awe. For she was not one of those "ugly Americans" we've read about, but a respectful, faithful woman who was interested in God's handiwork of creation and God's handiwork of diverse peoples.

Dorothy loved the world. In her own quiet way, we saw it when she spoke of the importance of our ELCA Global Mission Events. Ten, I believe, is the number of mission events she and Virginia attended through the years.

Global Mission was her passion. And she rejoiced when the people of St. John's would catch on to its importance, whether it was in support of Laurie Meyer, our missionary in Tanzania, or in support of the "Missionary for a Day" program. And when we began talking about St. John's

"For God So Loved the World"

entering into a partnership with a congregation in Tanzania, it brought a smile of anticipation to her face.

In the four and a half years that I have been pastor here, I have been greeted by Dorothy with a smile every time we met. This very private person would let me enter into her world with a feeling of welcome. We'd sometimes share a funny story and she'd chuckle and the jowls of her face and her whole body would shake. She was always glad to be with you folks, to expand her world by entering yours, to show her appreciation that you could share the world together.

Dorothy loved the world, from that South Dakota prairie, where she grew up and where her ashes will be buried, to that place in Turkey, where she heard the sounds from the minaret calling Muslims to worship; from the grandeur of the Great Wall in China to the sacred places where Jesus walked in the Holy Land. She loved the world and the world's people.

I have chosen the most familiar verses from the third chapter of John because they are about love for the world—God's love for the world—for the seas and the plains, for the mountains and the valleys, for this terra firma that gives us a sense of place and possibility, for this earth we call home. You see, it says, "God so loved *the world.*" The whole created order. Not simply the human family, but the very

In the Hollow of God's Hand

place where the human family lives and works and plays, the place of birds and carnivores, of whales and mosquitoes, the place of flora and fauna, the place where God's Son came to be born and live among us and where God calls us to love the world, too. Love it in all its wonder and in all its pain, in all its glory and in all its tears, in all its uniqueness and in all its diversity.

God's Son was sent into the world, not to condemn the world, but that the world might have life in Jesus' name. That life is life today, captured by mystery, captured by wonder, captured by love.

Dorothy's life celebrated in her own way the larger world of God's making. May we be caught by that vision, too, and become passionate about loving this world that God so loves. Amen

Jim
Age 87

WHERE DOES ONE BEGIN? With talk of his service in the military and his help in starting an American Legion Post? With his donating his body to research so that others may be helped through the advancement of medical study?

Let me begin at a senior citizens' dinner at Zion. That is where I first met Jim. I was new to Iowa City in the fall of 1980 and was meeting lots of folks. I had met his wife at a Table Communion Service some time before. At that senior citizens' dinner, she introduced me to Jim, whom I would see on numerous occasions at such gatherings. (That was as close to the sanctuary as I'd ever see him.)

In the Hollow of God's Hand

I remember the smile on his face, the way he enjoyed himself. I'd learn later that Jim was quite a salty fellow. In fact, his colorful language at times reminded me of my dad's. It fit him well, and somehow was a part of that strong, vibrant, spark-filled kind of life that was his.

I'd learn later of his love for books. Of the volumes that filled the shelves in the house on F Street. I learned that when Jim was a young man, some people thought he would become a doctor, which of course he didn't, or a teacher, which, I suspect, he did become more than he ever realized. Those books, those thousands of hours spent reading, helped to shape a person, to mold him, to enable him to experience lots of worlds. And learning from those worlds, he enlarged his own world for himself and for others. Maybe it was the Michener novels or the westerns or the thousands of short stories he absorbed. Whatever it was, he was molded into a man of strength and tenderness, of wisdom and faithfulness—a man worth his salt.

Some years ago, I heard a folk song about farmers by Buffy Sainte-Marie. The first stanza goes like this: "Men of the fields, men of the valleys, men of the seasons and the soil; strong hearts and hands molding the lands, all over earth they toil."

Jim was one of them. He loved to sit on his tractor and work it through the fields. He loved to care for the livestock,

A Man Worth His Salt

to take an interest in them, to watch them grow. He loved to make the land productive and nurture a flower in a garden. And Jim gave himself to those he loved. He loved to see them grow, too—wife and son and daughters and all the grandkids that were to follow.

From a difficult and painful childhood, there blossomed a man who vowed to live differently from the example he had seen in his own father. "I couldn't live like that," he told me once. And so he didn't. Rather, with strength and tenderness, wisdom and faithfulness, he shared a deep sense of love and caring for those around him, a deep sense of love and caring that helped you grow as children to adulthood with the support you needed to come into your own, to reach for those goals that were meaningful to you. Jim's pride in you, his love for you, his commitment to you are the signs of every teacher worth his salt, and Jim was salty.

This day our sadness is not consumed with, "If only we had done this or that for Jim or with him." Our sadness comes from the emptiness we all feel. The life of one of God's caring people is stilled. Suddenly and without warning, his heart gave out.

And in this moment, especially, the God who cares for us, the God who cares for all creation, providing for us so that we are not in want, this God is present to walk with us

In the Hollow of God's Hand

through the valley of death's shadow, so we are not afraid. This God comes to bring peace to troubled hearts and minds as we continue our journey.

We continue our journey in confidence because of that event we celebrated just last Sunday—Easter. Because Christ lives, we too shall live. That is God's promise to us all. One day we too, having died, shall break the bonds of death by the power of God to live forever with our God and with each other, molded and shaped in God's image.

It is that image that we continue to reclaim in our journey on earth as we grow in love for each other, in caring for family and friends and for all peoples of the world, so that one day all may experience the love of God and we will all lift up our voices together and say:

"Our Father who art in heaven, hallowed be thy name, thy kingdom come, thy will be done, on earth as it is in heaven. Give us this day our daily bread; and forgive us our trespasses, as we forgive those who trespass against us; and lead us not into temptation, but deliver us from evil. For thine is the kingdom, and the power, and the glory, forever and ever. Amen"

Farrell
Age 87

IF YOU WERE EVER WITH FARRELL when he got started on stories from the war, you had better be prepared to "set a piece." He was in his element then.

The stories would flow. About the European Campaign of World War II. About the Battle of the Bulge. About serving in the communications/signal corps. About the food he made for the soldier's mess. About his buddies. About how tough it was. About how tough they had to be. About how scary it could get. About the celebration when the war ended. About the long, long trip back home.

In the Hollow of God's Hand

If you were ever with him when he got started on stories from the war, you'd better be prepared to "set a piece."

You know, when you're in the military in time of war, you begin to understand things that others have difficulty with. You get to know what it means to live with someone else giving orders. You get to know how important commands are and how obeying them is critical in battle, and how following them can save your life and the lives of others. You get to know, too, what it means when someone lays down his or her life for somebody else, especially a friend. And what it means to take risks on behalf of others. You get to know, too, something deep about friendship that is forged in battle. And, finally, you get to know what real sadness is when you lose a buddy. And what true joy is when victory is finally won.

Today's gospel from the fifteenth chapter of John is not a metaphor for military life, but it does speak of how one lives in the relationship that God has established with us. And how that relationship is ordered, not chaotic; disciplined, not lax. And how there is One who leads, and there are commands and expectations and risks.

We remember that Jesus chose us, not the other way around. We recall that we were chosen to bear the kinds of fruit that last, the fruits of love. We remember that those fruits of love come out of a disciplined life, a life committed

The Disciplined Life

and dedicated, a life that knows that we demonstrate our love for God by walking in those commands of God. We recall that the greatest love of all is the love that lays itself down for one's friends. And we find the name of Jesus written all over that verse and all over us. We remember that Jesus called his followers friends as they faced the daily battle. We recall that Jesus speaks God's good word to us so that we might know the joy of being loved by God and be filled with the joy of Jesus Christ.

All of us who knew Farrell knew him as a man of joy who laughed easily and had a zest for life. He was the kind of fellow who loved to engage you in conversation, even if you were meeting for the very first time. The kind of fellow who enjoyed a good time and a good joke. The kind of warm, inviting fellow who smiled at you when he gave you a bulletin at church, who made you glad to be with him.

Some of you remember him as that young man who played outfield and second base for the Des Moines Zephyrs semipro ball club years ago, or as one who loved to cheer on the Hawkeyes and who would stick with the Cubs through thick and thin—and there was a lot of thin.

Some of you remember him as that fellow who worked hard all those years at Younkers. Some of his neighbors remember him as the one they could count on when they needed help. Some of you remember the delight he took

In the Hollow of God's Hand

in his grandkids and great-grandkids. Some of you remember that he was always prompt, on time, reliable. Some of you remember a cheerful soul who loved to talk with you. Some of you remember that in tough times, he was not afraid; in hard times, he remained upbeat. Even in intensive care, as one thing after another went wrong and all around were anxious, Farrell remained calm.

Today, I remember a man with a glow in his face and a tear of love in his eye as he talked about his grandkids. I remember a man faithfully at his post as a second service usher—smile on his face, eager to make others feel welcome at St. John's. I remember a man directing communicants to receive the Lord's Supper, and when others were all done, bringing up the end of the line. He would kneel, hands out to receive the sacrament and head nodding up and down, as if to say of it, "Yes, yes."

We all remember Farrell as friend. And that's how Jesus remembers him, too. Today, the promises of Jesus for all whom he calls friends are these: "I am the resurrection and the life. Because I live, you will live also." "I am with you always," in wartime, in peace time, forever. Amen

Gladys
Age 89

Gladys talked of Sunday School classes years ago, of playing the organ and trying to figure out how to lead the congregation in the liturgy when she didn't understand the Norwegian the pastor was speaking and singing. She talked of reading for the minister. "Train up a child in the way she should go …" There is no doubt that Gladys was trained up in the faith.

Her well-worn Bible spoke of the classes and study she had done through the years, working late into the night, reading the Bible and checking commentaries and Bible dictionaries. She was in her prime at the Friday afternoon study. She loved to ask questions, loved to see if the pastor was as prepared as she. It was always a challenge, especially when some of her questions would intentionally take us far afield and she might share a bit of special knowledge that she had gleaned from her late night reading. "Train up a child …"

That training brought her to Zion years ago where she staked her place in the sanctuary. I can still see her arriving just a tad late to worship, walking down the aisle next to the organ and sliding into the end seat of the sixth pew. It didn't matter if someone was sitting there, she just shoved them down a bit to claim her space.

I suspect it was that kind of forcefulness and fortitude that most of us remember Gladys for, when she worked as church secretary and then as security guard. Given Gladys's gumption and her propensity for taking charge, folks responded by either loving her or staying out of her way.

I am tempted today to use as my text Matthew 16:19 when Jesus says, "Behold, I give you the keys of the kingdom." We all know that Gladys had a key to everything. I once inadvertently locked my rolltop desk at home. I mentioned it, and that evening she led me through her tightly packed kitchen and into the living room, where she sat me down and dumped into my lap hundreds of keys. And I found one that did the trick.

Keys to the Kingdom

Yes, Gladys had keys for everything including the church, "the kingdom," we might call it. *Her* kingdom, she thought. And she let everybody know, in no uncertain terms, how everything ought to be in place and cared for. One doesn't endear oneself to folks that way, but that didn't bother her, for her task was to guard the kingdom.

And she did, armed with flashlight and wooden club that she stuck in the ribs of more than one itinerant she found sleeping in the pews. Yes, she did, making sure the children knew how they ought to behave in the church and scaring the "bejeebers" out of some of them. Late at night she would make her rounds, checking everything from windows to doors to furnaces to appliances, seeing that everything was in its place.

It was a very cold, snowy January Saturday about five years ago. Time for 5:15 worship and nobody made it but Gladys, who had forged her way across the street using an ice chipper to keep her from falling. There the two of us were. We did the confession of sin. We sang hymns. I preached the sermon. We shared communion. The full worship service. Afterwards, we laughed over the old story of the farmer who had only one hog who came to the trough. "He didn't feed the hog the whole feed load, you know," she jibed.

But the years took their toll, and Gladys was moved to

a care center. When the funeral director called the other day to tell me Gladys had died, I spent the next few hours in great sadness, remembering those conversations in front of her house as she leaned on a broom handle and smoked those unfiltered Camels held in her own plastic filter. Remembering her all decked out in her finery and jewelry, getting in that Caddy to go for an outing. Remembering her jaunts into Saturday night worship, often late because she couldn't leave the TV until the game was completely over. Remembering the people she helped with their finances because she was always good with numbers. Remembering the times when we had sharp words of disagreement about any number of issues, but always remained friends.

"Train up a child … and when she is old she will not depart from it." Gladys lived that verse. She stuck with the faith because she knew a God who stuck with her through thick and thin. A God who is *for* us humans. A God who came to live in our midst, to love us and care for us, to watch over us and comfort us, and to give us the keys of the kingdom as we journey through this world and reach for the world to come. Amen

ERCELL
Age 89

"There is a time to plant," the writer of Ecclesiastes tells us. Ercell loved to plant—flowers, bushes, trees, you name it. Maybe up to two hundred different plants, his son-in-law said the other day, including that grapefruit tree planted eleven years ago at their home in New Port Richey, a tree yielding the sweetest-tasting grapefruit your mouth could savor.

"There is a time to plant." As I thought of Ercell's love of planting and gardening, I asked myself why, and wondered if it didn't have something to do with his early childhood, when his parents were always on the move. He was a

In the Hollow of God's Hand

young boy who ended up attending twelve different schools, not able to put down roots, not able to be really planted in a place and stay there.

"There is a time to plant." No wonder he wanted to settle down, to get planted for a while in one place. After five years of farming, Ercell and Maurine moved to Des Moines and stayed for almost forty years, and then moved to Florida some twenty years ago. And, of course, most notable, lived sixty-six years together as husband and wife, an important role model for our society today.

"There is a time to plant." You know, planting is not easy work. It's hard. And Ercell was a hard worker. He was diligent in providing for his family—working hard at farming, then working double shifts at the tire factory, then driving a bread truck and food truck and school bus.

When you're settling in and building a family and home, it takes work. It takes time, this planting your roots, so you and those you love can grow.

"There is a time to plant." Almost fifty years ago, Pastor Fred Weertz here at St. John's saw that something needed to be planted in Ercell's life—a word, a living word, a word from God, a word of forgiveness, a word of salvation, a word of hope. And it was planted in Ercell and at age thirty-nine, almost forty, he was baptized into the Christian faith here at St. John's.

"A Time to Plant"

"There is a time to plant." Planting is also quiet work. And Ercell was a quiet man. Perhaps that's why he enjoyed his time in the garden, laying in the seed or the young bushes or plants, and then watching them grow, seeing the fruit of his hands blossom and bring delight to him and those around him.

"There is a time to plant." When you think about it, planting is what we are doing all our lives—planting seeds. Ercell planted the seeds of love, of kindness, of generosity, of hard work. His family and friends could see it in his smile, in the caring way he held his twenty-five grandkids, great-grandkids, and great-great-grandkids or played with them or teased them. And in his love for Maurine.

"There is a time to plant." I want to go back to that grapefruit tree, planted and nurtured, that yields such sweet grapefruit. In some ways, it is a picture, a metaphor of Ercell's life, a life yielding good fruit. No wonder Jesus reminds us, "By their fruit, you will know them." You will know the believers.

"There is a time to plant." Today, God is at work, right here in this place, planting something in us called hope. Hope that is able to see beyond death. Hope that is confidently able to face the loss of one we loved and know that God will walk with us into tomorrow, and we are not alone. Hope that clings tenaciously to the promise of Jesus planted today, here, in us: "I am the resurrection and the life." "Because I live, you will live also," today, tomorrow, forever. Amen

Francis Lee
Age 90

THE HEADLINE IN THE Des Moines Register a few days ago had it right. It read, "Jazzman 'Cigar' Bates just 'had it' in him." And what was "it"? That sense of rhythm, that love of life, that delight in playing, that fun in performing, that engaging humor, that joy in simply being alive.

Whether you were watching him on stage or playing along with him or simply having a conversation together, he had that good energy that made you glad you were with him.

Even after he had a stroke last Saturday, his spirit shone through. I walked into his hospital room on Sunday and

Eunice said, "Dad, Pastor Nilsen is here." And his reply was, "Yeah, the Milwaukee Kid." We shared a Milwaukee bond. And there he was, critically ill, remembering, enjoying, and making me glad I knew him.

I suspect we are all here this afternoon because we all shared a bond with this good man, this gifted man, this loving man, this funny man.

I remember the Martin Luther King, Jr., observance here at St. John's a few years ago. The choir and congregation had sung a few African American spirituals. After church, Francis said, "You know, it almost sounded like black folk singing here today in our very white church." And then with a twinkle in his eye and a smile on his face, he added, "Almost."

Sometimes God puts people in our lives or lets them cross our paths to show us something most important. Francis was one of those people, and I think he was meant to help us all see and experience joy.

Jesus said, "As the Father has loved me, so I have loved you; abide in my love. If you keep my commandments, you will abide in my love just as I have kept my Father's commandments and abide in his love. I have said these things to you so that my joy may be in you, and that your joy may be complete."

Francis just had it in him. You could see that joy written

He Just Had It in Him

in his smile and as he clenched that familiar stogie in his teeth. You could see it in the way he treated others with respect and how he would take time for family and friends. You could see it as he played that bass so his whole body moved and throbbed and the joy just poured out of him. You could even sense the joy when it was shrouded with grief, when he experienced the death of his own son, Abdula, a couple of years ago.

The world has way too much sadness and not nearly enough joy. And so when we see joy, when we find it alive and well, when we detect it in a rhythmic beat, when we catch it in a gracious smile, when we behold it in a warm greeting, we try to hold on to it, to remember it, and most of all, to share it.

That's what Christian living is all about—sharing what we have in us. That soul-filled music. That capacity to love, to give, to brighten someone's life, to lighten someone's burden. That joy that comes when we know we are loved, loved by Jesus Christ who seeks to give us his joy, so that our joy may be complete.

Today, sadness has intruded itself into our lives. We grieve Francis's death. We will miss his presence. We will miss his music. But sadness will not win the day. For we will remember Jazzman "Cigar" Bates. Our feet will tap to the rhythms we heard from him. Our memories will hold on to

In the Hollow of God's Hand

the humor we shared. Our hearts will beat with the love he gave. Our spirits will soar with the joy he lived.

Sadness will not win the day. Death will not carry this day. For we hold tenaciously to the One who promises, "I am the resurrection and the life." "Because I live, you shall live, also." We hold to the God who lived close to our friend Francis and lives close to us. We hold to God's Son, Jesus Christ, from whom *all* joy comes. We hold to this Jesus who promises that his joy will be in us so that our joy may be complete.

And if we listen closely, we just might hear Jazzman "Cigar" Bates tunin' up with all those other heavenly musicians, gettin' ready to play, "O when the saints go marchin' in, when the saints go marchin' in, O Lord, I want to be in that number, when the saints go marchin' in." Let's sing it!

WEST
AGE 91

I STAND BEFORE YOU, seeing the grief on your faces over the loss of your father and grandfather, friend and companion. A grief mellowed over the years as Alzheimer's disease began, little by little, robbing you of the man you had known. A grief filled with memories of what once was, of the man who once lived and loved, of the knowledge and wisdom gone forever.

Two thousand years ago, in the midst of a grieving family, Jesus came to bring hope. You may remember the story: Mary, Martha, and Lazarus were sisters and brother, living together in Bethany, and Jesus was so close, he was like family to them. When Jesus arrives after Lazarus's death, Martha is upset with him because he hasn't come sooner. Jesus says, Martha, look at me. "I am the resurrection and the life." Martha, hope is not only about some future time, hope is right here. Right now. In the love of your sister and friends.

Later Jesus would perform a miracle and raise Lazarus from the dead, but before that happened, he performed a miracle in Martha's heart. He gave her hope, not just for her reunion with her brother in the resurrection, but also for her life now, her life still blessed with family and friends.

God has always worked in families. From the beginning of time, we read of Abraham and Sarah and their children, Isaac and Rebekah and their children, Jacob and Rachel and their children. The landscape of both the Old and New Testaments finds God at work in families, at work to give hope, at work to demonstrate love, at work to enable us to discover how to live.

Think of all that family has meant to West. How he taught you to enjoy family, to take care of one another, to love one another, to provide for one another. And how in these later years, you have cared for him just as he taught you to care for others.

I have always been intrigued by a verse from Psalm 68. In the King James Version it reads, "God setteth the solitary

The Gift of Family

into families." God acts to create the environment that can give security and love and care. God acts to create the environment that can give us hope for today and for tomorrow.

How different life would be if we had to live solitary lives, without the benefit of all that family gives us. I remember when I was a teen years ago, I was furious about something, so I decided to run away from my home in Milwaukee and go to Chicago. I boarded the bus and traveled south. But when I got there and began walking around the bus depot, I became frightened. Even when I didn't like my parents very much, I always felt safe and cared for. I knew I belonged. So I got back on the bus and went home. There I was greeted by a weeping mother and an angry father. But it was home. And, grounded in my room, I had a lot of time to think about the importance of family.

The Bible is clear that we are not made to be solitary figures, we are meant to be in family, in community.

No wonder the faith community is called the family of God. We need one another. And in belonging to one another, we discover who God is and what God is about in this world. Faith is given birth here—in the family. And love is practiced here—in the family. And hope grows here—in the family, equipping us to live fully in God's world, knowing we live better together than alone.

In the Hollow of God's Hand

West took family very seriously. He showed you how important it was, how it shaped people and relationships in ways nothing else can. He committed himself to providing the stability that children need in their growing years. He committed himself to seeing that the children got an education. He committed himself to teaching all of you to love each other and also to make that love so strong that it would give you hope in the midst of life's sadness.

In these past years, as West's mind gradually gave way to Alzheimer's disease, I suspect that you, his children, often found yourselves wondering how Dad would do something or what he would think. And I suspect that you, his grandchildren, often wondered how he would deal with some situation or some person or what he might think about some issue you were struggling with. I suspect that he's often been present, right there with you, even when miles and time separated you. That's what happens when family means much. And he will continue to be with you, in your memories, in your thoughts, in your hopes.

Just as Jesus was present with the family of Mary and Martha and Lazarus to give security and hope in the face of death, so his promise is to be with us, not in some resurrection some day, but *now,* wrapping his arms around us and saying, "I am the resurrection and the life." For you. For today. Live in me and hope will never die. Amen

Helene
Age 91

IN THE FUNERAL LITURGY of the Orthodox Prayer Book, there are a number of anthems set to different musical tones to be chanted by the priest or choir. Hear the words of Tone VI. They form a prayer, acknowledging God as Creator and a plea for entrance into eternal rest in the "land of the living."

"Thy creative command was my origin and my existence, for it was thy pleasure, out of visible and invisible ingredients, to fashion me as a living creature. Thou hast shaped my body from the earth, and thou hast given me a soul by thy divine and quickening breath. Wherefore, O

In the Hollow of God's Hand

Christ, give rest unto thy servant in the land of the living and in the abodes of the just."

I can hear the prayer as if our friend, Helene, who was born and raised in St. Petersburg, Russia, was speaking it. I can hear her praying it when the Iron Curtain came tumbling down. When the dramatic changes in Russian society began to take place. When religion began to show itself in fresh ways in that land. At that time, Professor Helene Scriabine said, "Yes, even the politicians claim religion now. How ironic."

Set back from Nevsky Prospect in St. Petersburg is St. Peter Lutheran Church, built to serve German Lutherans in St. Petersburg some time after the turn of the century. During the Second World War, the political regime turned it into a public natatorium—a swimming pool. A hole was dug into the main floor. An indoor pool created. Bleachers for spectators were set on three sides. And at the end, a high dive was erected where once stood the high altar and cross.

In June 1995, my wife and I stood in that place, soon to be renovated to become a place of worship again. Annie, a resident of St. Petersburg, told us how her family used to come here to swim, as did many families. And she said, "You know, a family would gather, parents and children together in the pool. And sometimes, if there was a young baby, when the lifeguards were not watching close, one of the parents, holding the baby, with the others circled about, would take water and put it on the head of the baby, while saying the words, 'You are baptized in the name of the Father, and of the Son, and of the Holy Ghost.' "

By innovative means, the faith survived in the lives of many in that great land where faith was suppressed for so long. And faith lives on in the hearts of many today.

In the fourth volume of *Coming of Age in the Russian Revolution,* Helene tells of the burial of her grandmother in March of 1917, and the air of foreboding in her family. She writes, "The evening after the burial, Father said, as if to himself, not turning to anyone in particular, 'With Mama they have buried the old world. This world has gone forever. What does the future have in store for us?' "

For Helene and her family, a life of pain, loss, and separation: The Bolshevik Revolution. Civil War. The rise of Soviet power. The purges and terror of Stalin. The Nazi attack on Leningrad. The nine-hundred-day siege. The death of millions by hunger and malnutrition. Flight across the frozen Lake Lagoda. Internment in a foreign workers' camp in Germany. Liberation by the Allies in 1945. The death of her husband following the war, before he could know that Helene and their sons had survived.

There was emigration to America in 1950. Menial work

In the Hollow of God's Hand

in the early days. Then teaching Russian in Syracuse, earning her doctorate, and finally, from 1960 on, teaching at the University of Iowa.

The old world was gone, as her father had said that day in 1917. But Helene survived. She would have to shape a new world and new friendships. And that is what she did. That is why we are here, living testimony to her new world, new friendships, new life.

Helene's new life was still marked with a touch of the aristocracy of her younger days and fueled by fury toward both the Communists and the Nazis. It was a life that had passed through the valleys of deep shadows, a life shaped by those shadows long after the new day had dawned.

In her later life, she used to sit in the balcony here at Zion with a friend who brought her, since there was no Russian Orthodox church near. Or at the Methodist church, where another friend brought her. But I knew her mostly from our conversations. We would sit for hours in her house on Park Road, eating cakes and drinking tea, talking of her life, her youth, her struggles, her faith.

Not long ago, at Mercy Hospital, as she held stubbornly on to life, I prayed over her, "Lord, now let your servant depart in peace." She was not a perfect servant, not one without flaws, as you all well know. But she struggled with faith and tried to be faithful. The icon on the stand next to her hospital bed gave testimony to the faith that survived in this survivor.

She survived. She survived more than most of us can ever imagine. And she learned to thrive. Maybe that is the lesson we can all learn from Helene's life as we walk through our own deep shadows.

God would have us not only survive, but thrive. And God promises to be at our side through the struggle, through the valley of shadows. The One who has given us life, whose creative command has been our origin, the One who has fashioned us as living creatures, shaping our bodies from the earth and breathing the divine into our souls, that God calls us to live fully and abundantly in God's goodness and grace.

And so we pray confidently in the words of the prayer found in the Orthodox liturgy, "O Christ, give rest unto thy servant in the land of the living and in the abodes of the just." Amen

Van
Age 91

I'VE ALWAYS LIKED A MAN with strong convictions. I guess that's because my dad was like that. He knew what he thought and why he thought it. He knew what he believed and why he believed it. And he'd tell you.

It wasn't long after I arrived at St. John's that I discovered Van to be just such a man. Sitting in the lounge after service one Sunday, he let me know in no uncertain terms, "The organ is too loud." He thought I should take care of it right then and there, because a few Sundays later, balancing on his two canes, he caught my attention and forcefully reminded me, "The organ is still too loud, and it does terrible things to my hearing aids."

In the Hollow of God's Hand

So my first impression was, here's a fellow who's not afraid to let me know what is on his mind. And I might have cringed about all this, but while visiting at Methodist Hospital one time, not long after that, when I called him his given name, "Wally," he said to me, "Call me Van. My friends do." And it felt good. The Parkinson's disease that left his limbs shaking did not affect his sturdy spirit.

You know, it's hard to dislike anybody who has a cap that says on it, "I'm always right," because you know he has a sense of humor about himself. My dad had a T-shirt he loved to wear that took that thought even a bit further. It said, "I'm always right, even when I'm wrong." I have a feeling Van could have had a lot of fun with that shirt.

But when it came to a discussion of politics or the stock market or economics or maybe even religion, Van certainly could be intimidating to a novice who didn't have his or her arguments all thought out.

Van was a product of the Great Depression. And when your family loses everything, it can give you an appreciation for the simple things in life and cause you to trim down your needs. If you have things, you might lose them again, and you don't want to risk that pain over and over again. It can also cause you to look at things somewhat conservatively. And maybe those depression years really do form you for the rest of your life and give you strong convictions about how best to live that life.

Winifred shared with me that Van didn't have much schooling. He was mostly self-taught. As a youth and young man, he always had a dictionary beside his bed, learning on his own, developing a good vocabulary, wrestling with definitions and meanings of words worth thinking about, and then using them to persuade others.

That might be a reason he was so successful selling law books and tax books for Prentice-Hall. You have to know how to sell to stay in that business for twenty years. Not only do you have to have a pleasing way about you, but you have to know how to convince, how to persuade your potential customer to buy. And very often Van was among the best salesmen for Prentice-Hall in the country.

So, here a man comes to the close of his life, and we are grateful for his life, for his many years. But looking back at that life, we also ask a question, "Where is God in all these ninety-one years?" For Van, God sat at the center of life, and the church was God's body. St. John's was a part of who he was—always at worship, years spent ushering, getting his boys to Sunday School and confirmation and into the Order of St. John's and the bell choir. And praying together with his wife at night, when he wasn't on the road selling.

It's good to see a man with strong convictions in the church, even when you don't agree with him, a man who led by example, a man who dared to live simply in a society that is all about consumption, a man of faith.

The Bible tells us about another such man. Born poor, he lived simply. But he had such a strong head and strong convictions that when others told him to take care of himself and not go to Jerusalem, because that would only mean trouble, he went anyway. And there gave his life for his friends—for humanity.

It is this strong-willed man of strong convictions whom Van knew and whom we know as Jesus. And this Jesus promises to be with us through the most difficult days, promises that death is not the end of our story—even at ninety-one years.

Instead, Jesus promises, "I am with you," and "I am the resurrection and the life." "Because I live, you shall live also." Today we can all count on that. For Jesus—this man of strong convictions—never breaks a promise. And besides that, we know that he is truly always right. Amen

Stella Mae
Age 93

ON THE VERY FIRST SUNDAY I was here at St. John's, a little over a year ago, I reached out to greet her as she was leaving. "My name is Stella Mae," she told me. "Not Stella. Stella Mae." I knew right then and there that here was a woman who was sure of herself. She knew who she was and, boy, the new pastor ought to get it right from the beginning.

This past Friday evening we were together at Calvin Manor. She had a little trouble recognizing me at first, her eyesight had gotten so bad, but when she did, she told me, "Stella Mae isn't doing very well." We talked about her illness for a while, about how her body was shutting down one organ at a time. And then we talked about her readiness to die. "Well," she said, "I've lived a long life and it has been a good life. But I'd like to live a little longer, if possible. There's still more I'd like to do."

Well, Stella Mae didn't get to do more. She died on Saturday. But what a life she lived. What gifts she offered. What lessons she taught.

The passage from Revelation tells us, "Here is a call for the endurance of the saints, those who keep the commandments of God and hold fast to the faith of Jesus."

Stella Mae had endurance. That small girl raised in Buffalo Center, Iowa, stretched herself. From the bachelor's degree she worked hard to receive from St. Olaf College to the master's degree she earned at the University of Colorado, Stella Mae was about learning, about growing.

From all the classes she taught in social studies and instrumental music in small towns and then in Des Moines, Stella Mae was about teaching, about having a passion for kids, about working with them to learn and learn and learn some more.

Stella Mae's niece told me that Stella Mae was so dedicated to her students that she simply "wanted to save them all," to make sure they knew more after they had her as a teacher than before, to make sure they developed to be good citizens of good character.

"Still More I'd Like to Do"

We all know how much endurance it takes to be a teacher—class preparation, teaching, grading tests, interacting with students, trying to give each one personal attention, relating to their parents and families.

Stella Mae had that kind of endurance. Maybe it was because of her strict Norwegian Lutheran upbringing. I don't know. But she stuck with kids, even when it wasn't easy to do so.

And she stuck with her Lord, through thick and thin. A faithful follower of Jesus who knew she was loved by God, Stella Mae lived with a sense of confidence that comes to a person who knows she is loved.

Sunday after Sunday she made sure she got to church to worship the One she knew loved her. Sunday after Sunday she gave witness to her faithfulness to a God who was faithful to her.

Day after day, she witnessed to that faithfulness, too, as she taught and taught and taught about a world larger than just an individual, a world where people relate to one another and societies flourish or fall. Social studies, they called it then, were the classes about how people live together, and Stella Mae instilled a notion about how that could be done to the benefit of all.

Day after day she witnessed as she helped students learn music, as she acquainted them with one of the great gifts

In the Hollow of God's Hand

God has given to humanity—music that can free our spirits. That can lift us up. That can stir the heart and bring beauty within our grasp so we can almost touch the face of God.

And so we sing many hymns today and listen to the sounds of harp and organ and find ourselves lifted up before God's throne of grace by music, in the same way that Stella Mae was. And we sing the keynote song of the St. Olaf Choir, "Beautiful Savior," remembering the school she so dearly loved, a school with the Christian church at its heart.

So, today, we say thanks to God for Stella Mae. For how she touched our lives with caring and humor, how she witnessed to her faith in worship and work, how she held fast to her faith in Jesus.

And we celebrate that she is at rest in the presence of God, at rest from her labors. And for this saint, we say, "Thanks be to God who gives us the victory through our Lord Jesus Christ." Amen

Leora
Age 95

JOHN 3:16 WAS LEORA'S FAVORITE VERSE, as it is the favorite verse of many Christians. "For God so loved the world that he gave his only begotten Son, that whoever believes in him should not perish, but have everlasting life." She learned it at a young age and knew it by heart, so it could give her comfort and strength in times of need.

"Please read John 3:16 to me," Leora said some years ago when her pastor stopped by her hospital bed. As he read those familiar words, she recited them by heart along with him. It was part of her, like her love of those two hundred rose bushes she planted and fussed over at the

In the Hollow of God's Hand

house on 52nd Street. Like her commitment to learning and education and knowing their importance for her children. Like her devotion to her children and grandkids and great-grandkids and her enjoyment in caring for them.

"For God so loved the world ..." But do you remember what follows? Have you committed to memory the next verse? Leora had. She could take you to the heart of the Christian faith spelled out in the next verse, in verse 17. Listen to it: "For God sent not his Son into the world to condemn the world, but that the world through him might be saved."

Sound vaguely familiar? God isn't about condemning the world, but saving it. Not about putting us down, but raising us up. Not about punishing, but about freeing. Not about death, but about life.

How refreshing to talk with someone who can give us this picture of a God worth believing in. A God who is *for* humanity, not against humanity. A God in whom there is real reason to hope—for today, for tomorrow, forever. And Leora knew such a God.

And, you know, if that is your starting place in life, if that is what your life is rooted in, it gives you a whole different perspective about living. It frees you to embrace life in all its beauty and wonder and possibilities and to invest

A God Worth Believing In

your life, as God has done, in the creation and in others, and to savor the joy of seeing them grow and flourish.

When I think of the creation, I picture God taking lots of time. I know the first chapter of Genesis talks about creation in six days. But like the apostle Peter, I have a hunch that "a day is like a thousand years" and that with each of those long days God savored what was being created, savored the beauty, the magnificence, the wonder of it all— the waters, the night and the day, the sun and moon and stars, the dry land, the vegetation, the fish, the birds, the animals, and finally humans. God took God's good-natured time about it. "For God so loved the world …"

You've got to take time to fuss over those two hundred rose bushes and to plant vegetables and wait for them to grow, as Leora did. It takes time and loads of love to teach four kids how to do needlework, can fruits and veggies, and set a nice table of food that is not only good to look at but scrumptious to eat. That takes time.

It takes time and loads of love to creatively teach kids how to spell and do math and learn words. So Leora devised puzzles and games and spelling bees to keep those young ones interested. And she sang hymns with them as the family would drive along the flatlands of Nebraska long ago.

"For God so loved the world" so that we would love it, too. And not only love our own families that mean so much to us and that we treasure deep in our hearts, but love the larger world of creation and the world of people. Leora knew that larger world—a world where people were hurting, a world where people were disadvantaged. Patients at Lutheran Hospital still have a flower cart that comes around to deliver flowers. That was Leora's idea years ago. She also taught women at the Home for the Blind to knit and crochet, and with Carl, built a stake and rope railing so blind people could take a walk outside in a wooded area. It all takes time and love.

We're drawing near to Christmas, and we'll celebrate the One who came into the world, the One who came to save the world, to make it whole, to give it life as God first gave it life in creation.

Today we celebrate Leora's life and even more we celebrate the reality of a God worth believing in, a God who loved the world so much that he gave his only begotten son so that the world through him might be saved. What a reason to celebrate! Amen

IRENE
AGE 95

HAVE YOU EVER WATCHED a weaver at work? Bent over a loom with shuttle in hand. Bringing threads together of different color and often different texture. Forming a marvelous pattern, perhaps a tapestry that tells a story of life.

Irene was a weaver, I understand. One who did exquisite work. Some of you have her work in your homes.

As I listened to you and learned about Irene just a few days ago, I saw threads woven together that tell, in a small way, the story of her life. A Drake graduate who earned her library degree at the University of Denver, Irene used her skills as a librarian.

She was the head librarian for Standard Oil in New York City for more than two decades. Life in New York gave her the opportunity to experience the marvelous world of theater and art galleries and opera from the thirties into the fifties. And she kept up those interests upon returning to Des Moines.

She loved to travel, to see as much of the world as she could. She loved to have people in for an evening. Threads woven together.

And then, not quite so glamorous, but just as important, there is also the well-thumbed Bible that was hers, that gives us a glimpse into her faith. And word is that she and her sister would often close an evening together in one or the other's apartment by praying the Lord's Prayer.

Threads of education, of adventure, of appreciation for the arts, of closeness to a sister, of faithfulness to her God all woven together to tell a story, the story of Irene's life.

I suspect that her many years were not all filled with grace and growing. There were times of hurt and pain. Times of struggle alongside times of peace. Times of sadness alongside times of joy. Life is like that—threads of all sorts get woven into the fabric of our story.

And while God provides the threads and the loom and the weaver's shuttle, it is we who get to weave the threads together, making a tapestry that tells the story of our days, of our lives.

Her gravestone will read: Irene Keefner, 1904–1999. And, you know, it's what she did with the dash that counts. Her dash was like a weaver's shuttle. And she wove together the threads she was given to make and live a beautiful life.

And so it is for us all. It's what we do with the dash that counts. How we weave the threads together to make and live a life. How we make a tapestry that tells the story of our days.

Will ours be informed by theater and art, by travel and entertaining? Will ours be informed by a well-thumbed Bible and by saying the Lord's Prayer at the close of the day, as was Irene's?

Maybe the story of our days will be informed by those evidences of God's love and grace and hope in our lives. Or maybe they will be informed by myriads of other possibilities. I hope it will be so, for these graces make the weaving of the tapestry so much more rich, the texture so much more beautiful.

And that is what God wants for us. In the resurrection of Jesus Christ, God makes possible a rich and textured life for us today and forever.

In the Hollow of God's Hand

Her last years were not easy, I'm told. Yes, the body grows old, is filled with aches and pains, and doesn't work as well as it once did. But now that is all past for her, and she is at peace, which is most appropriate, for "peace" is the meaning of her name, Irene. A peaceful weaver. A weaver of peace.

As we go from here to weave the rest of our lives, may we, by the power and promise of the Gospel, also be peaceful weavers and weavers of peace. Amen

Ralph
Age 95

HE WAS A DELIGHT! Stories abound about him and stories are what he loved to tell. Today we have heard some of the stories from his children, two of his grandchildren, and a friend, the president of Drake University, Dr. David Maxwell. "Bud," as we all knew him, would have gotten a kick out of those stories, a good laugh, and at the same time felt humbled by the gracious words spoken about him.

To those who knew him or knew of him, Dr. Dorner was larger than life. Not only his size, but his commitments, his dedication, his love of family, his integrity as a respected surgeon, his service for country as a major in the military in World War II, his support of Drake University and all the Bulldog teams, his faithful worship at St. John's, his participation in the Chamber of Commerce and in the Des Moines community to make it a better place. As his son, Doug, so aptly put it, like St. John's where he was a member, Dr. Dorner was "in the city for good."

And he enjoyed it all. I've never known such an avid poker player except for my own dad. Or a cribbage player who could beat you before you knew what was happening. Or an affluent doctor who used his own mimeographed sheet to score an Iowa Cubs game because, as he told me one night in the third-base box-seat section of the park, "The Cubs' play book costs too much."

Bud knew who he was. He had strong opinions. That's probably the understatement of the day. He knew where he stood. Religiously, professionally, politically. And that made him unafraid to voice what he had to say and also unafraid to tell a story that might make some folks squirm a bit.

I remember the third broadcast of the St. John's Forum over WOI a few years back. Gov. Vilsack was supposed to be the speaker, but his staff had messed up his schedule. So the First Lady of Iowa, Christie Vilsack, came in his place. Decked out in one of her most interesting hats, she talked about libraries, a passion of hers. And the importance

"God Be Praised! Hallelujah!"

of storytelling, too. When she finished, the announcer asked if there were any comments or questions. Dr. Dorner raised his hand and said, "I've got a story." He then proceeded to tell a slightly off-color story. When he delivered the punch line, you could see the pink rise in Mrs. Vilsack's face under her hat. The audience didn't know how to react at first, but then began to chuckle when everyone realized we were on WOI and Dr. Dorner's story had been broadcast for all of Iowa to hear. Bud was Bud and he knew who he was.

And Bud also knew *whose* he was. When he was hospitalized, I knew better than to make a pastoral call on him when a Cubs game was on. He wouldn't give me more than the time of day, then. But when the game was over, we could talk. And pray. And those larger-than-life hands would invite holding, as we called upon the God who had given him life, the God we now asked for healing.

We called upon the One whom he had so often invoked around his own family table by saying, "Lord, we thank you for the privilege of being together." The God he acknowledged to his family on the day his beloved Gene died by saying, "God was so good to us. God be praised! Hallelujah!" The One to whom he would often point after a difficult surgery when he would tell a family, "I did all I could do. Now it's in God's hands," and then often he would pray with them. The God whom Dr. Dorner regularly worshiped here, tooling into the sanctuary on his famous scooter this last year, when Doug or Ruthie would bring him to church in the van. As sharp as ever at ninety-five, a week ago Sunday he said, "Pastor, I especially liked the background in history you included today. It made the story much more clear." Later in that service, those larger-than-life hands took the bread and the wine, taking into his life the life of Jesus.

There was something in him—the spark of life, the love of life, the life of God.

Jesus said, "I came that they may have life and have it abundantly." Abundantly. Not in things, but in faith. Not in things, but in love. Not in things, but in people, in relationships, in friendships. Not in things, but in character and in service. Not in things, but in hope and joy.

Jesus' promise is offered to us all. Bud caught on to that. No wonder he had so much fun in life. No wonder he had so much dedication. No wonder he had so much vitality. And no wonder he was able to live so fully and die so well. No wonder you're all here—you saw it in him.

Jesus' word is still true today. "I came that they may have life and have it abundantly." Today, tomorrow, forever. We are here today to celebrate God, to celebrate a life, to celebrate life, to celebrate life together in the service of humankind. Now that's life worth living. God be praised! Hallelujah! Amen

MOTHER
Age 88

I BURIED MY MOTHER on Friday. The service was in a cemetery chapel in Milwaukee, her home town. There were just sixteen of us there. Most of the family has moved on and most of the old neighbors, too. So, we were ten family members, a few friends, and Joe, her old neighbor from next door. And God. God always seems to show up in times like that.

Our eldest son led the simple service, the kind Mom would have liked. "Amazing Grace" was sung, the Twenty-third Psalm read, prayers spoken, some funny stories about Mom were told. Even her great-grandson, Kristian, told about the chocolate treats they would always bring Great-Grandma, and how much she loved them. At the close of the short service we sang to Mom: "Jesus loves *you,* this we know." That's when Mary and I lost it. Our voices broke, our eyes pooled up, and I could feel an aching within.

I helped carry the casket out. The freshly dug grave was ready. My folks had chosen that plot in the cemetery under a tree, not far from a gently flowing stream. It was a peaceful place, they had told me, when they bought it fifty years ago. Dad has been there alone seventeen years. And now Mom is there, too. Our son led the burial service and I threw dirt on the casket as he said, "Earth to earth, ashes to ashes, dust to dust, in sure and certain hope of the resurrection to eternal life through our Lord Jesus Christ." And I could feel God's arms wrapped around me, sensing the aching in me, reminding me of the promise I had reminded so many others of throughout the years—the hope that belongs to all God's children.

After lunch and sharing of more "Mom" stories, we went back to the old neighborhood where the house she had lived in for fifty-five years still stands. The aching came back. The neighborhood has deteriorated a lot in the past few years—unpainted, unkempt houses, old cars (junkers, some of them) lining the street, unmown lawns, garbage strewn here and there, and people whose blank faces told

In the Hollow of God's Hand

us they were resigned to a life less than fulfilling. We took a few pictures of family on the steps in front of the old house—one last memento of other times—then said our farewells to one another and went our separate ways.

On the way out of town, Mary and I drove back to the cemetery. I wanted to see the grave filled in, make sure it was all taken care of. And it was. We took some of the flowers from the casket bouquet to bring home. I put my hand on the dirt. It felt good. "In sure and certain hope." The words came rushing back, and I could sense God's arms wrapped around me again.

"We are the children of God," Paul writes of us in Romans, "and if children, then heirs of God and joint heirs with Christ." And as heirs, we inherit everything—the bad with the good, the suffering with the glory.

No wonder the aching continues. I've noticed it growing in me. An aching because of the loss of my mom, sure, but I can't get the pictures of the old neighborhood out of my mind. It is an aching for people who are hurting, whose faces are blank, whose spirit is diminished. It is an aching with the earth as creation falls victim to exploitation and pollution and decay.

Sometime after we moved Mom to Des Moines, the parish nurse came to visit in her apartment. She wondered how Mom was doing during the transition to this new

In the Hollow of God's Hand

community after being uprooted from the place she had called home all her life. She told Mom the story of Abraham and Sarah leaving their home and setting out for a land God promised to show them, tenting along the way toward their destination. "Who do you feel most like in this story?" she asked. Mom thought a long time and then said, "I'm most like the tent. And my poles are getting shaky."

Just a week before she died, the parish nurse was with her again, this time in the nursing home. "How are you, Irene?" she asked. Remembering the story, Mom replied, "My poles are crumbling." A few days later, she died. Finally at rest, free from the pain the crumbling of her bones had caused. She was at peace.

Of course, I remember the times when she wasn't shaky or crumbling, but when she was strong, when her funny one-liners would crack us all up. When that spark of life radiated from her eyes as she held a grandchild on her lap or showed off her many pictures of them to anyone who would look. Or when she brought tears to our eyes as she prayed a humble prayer at our Christmas Eve family devotions.

But the aching I feel is not an aching that longs for the past, for what has been, for the good old days, but an aching that rushes to embrace the future for Mom and for all. Earth to earth, ashes to ashes, dust to dust, in sure and

In the Hollow of God's Hand

certain hope—a hope that brings beauty out of decay, a hope that renews purpose and restores people in a struggling community, a hope that brings life out of death.

As children of God, let us be bold to share the hope that is ours and the world's, knowing we are always held safe and secure in the hollow of God's almighty hand. Amen

INDEX OF TEXT REFERENCES

One or more of these texts were read during each service: Psalm 23, John 11:21–27, John 14:1–6, and I Cor. 15:51–57. In addition, the following texts informed individual sermons.

PAGE	NAME	TEXT
1	CAROL NOEL, 5	Mark 10:13–16
5	NICOLE, 10	John 15:9–11
9	PAMMY, 22	I John 4:7–12; Philippians 1:6
13	JOHN MICHAEL, 27	John 15:12–15; I Corinthians 13
17	ABDULA, 30	Deuteronomy 31:8
21	GREGORY, 34	Ecclesiastes 3:1–8
25	KENNETH, 37	II Timothy 4:7
29	BARBARA, 40	Psalm 121
35	STACIE, 42	John 15:9–11
39	MAVIS, 45	Ephesians 2:8–10
43	MARK, 46	Isaiah 40:29–31
47	JEAN, 53	II Corinthians 12:9–10
51	DON, 55	Psalm 26:1–3, 11–12

In the Hollow of God's Hand

55	**GEORGE, 56**	Matthew 28:20
59	**JEAN, 58**	Psalm 91:10–11
63	**NICK, 61**	Psalm 30:10–12; Isaiah 30:15
67	**NANCY, 63**	Psalm 25:4–10; John 14:27
71	**RUTH, 64**	Mark 10:13–16; I Thessalonians 5:17
75	**ART, 65**	Psalm 8
79	**LILA, 69**	Matthew 6:25–33
83	**DONALD, 70**	Romans 14:7–8
87	**BETTY, 73**	John 19:25–27a
91	**GINNY, 74**	Revelation 21:2–7
95	**DICK, 75**	John 10:11–18
99	**DON, 75**	John 6:16–21
103	**CARROLL, 76**	Isaiah 30:15
107	**JAMES, 76**	Isaiah 25:6; Jeremiah 29:11
111	**LEONARD, 79**	Galatians 5:22–25
115	**DONALD, 79**	John 15:11; Isaiah 41:10
119	**GEORGE, 80**	Philippians 4:4–7
123	**LESTER, 80**	Psalm 8; Psalm 46:1, 11

127	**PAT, 83**	Ecclesiastes 3:1–4; John 15:15
131	**GEORGE, 83**	Proverbs 11:2, 28:26b
135	**RUTH, 84**	Romans 8:31–35, 37–39
139	**MAYBELLE, 86**	Matthew 6:25–33; I Peter 1:24–25
143	**DOROTHY, 86**	John 3:16–17
147	**JIM, 87**	Mark 9:50
151	**FARRELL, 87**	John 15:9–15
155	**GLADYS, 89**	Matthew 16:19; Proverbs 22:6
159	**ERCELL, 89**	Ecclesiastes 3:1–2a
163	**FRANCIS LEE, 90**	John 15:9–12
167	**WEST, 91**	Psalm 68:6a
171	**HELENE, 91**	Revelation 2:10b; Luke 2:28–32
177	**VAN, 91**	Romans 8:31–35, 37–39
181	**STELLA MAE, 93**	Revelation 14:12
185	**LEORA, 95**	John 3:16–17
189	**IRENE, 95**	Ecclesiastes 3:1–8; Romans 8:31–35, 37–39
193	**RALPH, 95**	John 10:10b
197	**MOTHER, 88**	Romans 8:15b–17

Yea, though I walk through the valley
of the shadow of death,
I will fear no evil, for thou art with me.
Thy rod and thy staff they comfort me.
Psalm 23:4

"Let not your hearts be troubled ...
I go to prepare a place for you.
And if I go and prepare a place for you,
I will come again and will take you to myself,
so that where I am, there you may be also."
John 14:1–3

"I have said these things to you
so that my joy may be in you,
and that your joy may be complete."
John 15:11

"I am the resurrection and the life.
Those who believe in me,
even though they die, will live."
John 11:25

"Death has been swallowed up in victory."
"Where, O death, is your victory?
Where, O death, is your sting?" ...
But thanks be to God who gives us the victory
through our Lord Jesus Christ.
I Corinthians 15:54b-55, 57